GORDON RAMSAY'S ULTIMATE HOME COOKING

GORDON RAMSAY'S ULTIMATE HOME COOKING

HODDER & STOUGHTON

First published in Great Britain in 2013
by Hodder & Stoughton
An Hachette UK company

12

Copyright © Gordon Ramsay 2013

Programme, Programme Material and Format
copyright © One Potato Two Potato Limited 2012

Photography Copyright © Con Poulos 2013

A CIP catalogue record for this title is available from
the British Library

Hardback ISBN 978 1 444 78078 9
Ebook ISBN 978 1 444 78079 6

Typeset in Bembo and Futura

Design and art direction by James Edgar
at Post98design.co.uk

Printed and bound in Germany by
Mohn Media GmbH

Hodder & Stoughton policy is to use papers that are
natural, renewable and recyclable products and made
from wood grown in sustainable forests. The logging
and manufacturing processes are expected to
conform to the environmental regulations of the
country of origin.

Hodder & Stoughton would like to thank:
Bricket Davda (brickettdavda.com), Cutipol
(cutipol.pt), Folklore (shopfolklore.com),
Jia (jia-inc.com), Le Creuset (lecreuset.co.uk),
Mono (mono.de), and The Conran Shop
(conranshop.co.uk).

Hodder & Stoughton Publishers
Carmelite House
50 Victoria Embankment
London EC4Y 0DZ

www.hodder.co.uk

CONTENTS

INTRODUCTION

EVERYTHING I KNOW ABOUT COOKING I'VE LEARNT THROUGH HARD WORK, DRIVE AND PASSION.

From the age of 17 I made food my life, and it's fair to say that since then food has been the making of me. But the sort of cooking I made my name with – intricate dishes made with the world's finest ingredients – is a million miles from the food I cook at home. When I'm with friends and family I want things to be much more relaxed. I still want to use great ingredients, and to get the most from them, but my cooking becomes more rustic and easy-going.

That's not to say I'm not still using the techniques I apply in professional kitchens. The skills I learnt under some of the world's finest chefs, from Albert Roux to Guy Savoy, will stay with me for the rest of my life and I'd no more abandon them than I would open a greasy spoon. When you are a professional chef you apply all your knowledge instinctively – it's just that you have to apply it differently, because cooking at home throws up a different set of challenges. Hopefully your diners, be they friends or family, won't be expecting Michelin-quality cooking (if they are, they'll be sorely disappointed round at mine), but they can still be among the most demanding people to cook for, never afraid to tell you what they think.

So what do they and you want from home cooking? That's the first question to ask, and I think my answer is probably the same as it is in every house. With a busy family – there's me and Tana and our four children, Megan, Jack, Holly and Tilly – I want to be able to provide healthy food throughout the day, from breakfast to dinner, as quickly and efficiently as possible. I want it to be the kind of food that gets everyone excited, so there needs to be lots of variety. I want it to pack a punch, so I love big bold flavours. Above all, I want it to be the sort of food that will draw the whole family together. It really depresses me how many families don't eat as a unit any more, because, for me, sitting around a table sharing food and conversation is *the* biggest pleasure in life and a family that doesn't have that is all the poorer. But enough of the theory. Let's get on to the practice. How do you achieve all this?

I've divided this book into chapters to see you through the whole day, from weekday breakfasts through to Saturday night dinners, and hopefully you will find plenty of recipes that will become family favourites. But before we get on to those, let me share some general tips to make cooking a pleasure.

BE ORGANISED. After a lifetime in kitchens, this, I realise, is the golden rule. Nine times out of ten, if something goes wrong, it's your preparation that was at fault. Get your ingredients out, prep the vegetables, have all your pans ready and in easy reach. Not only will it make your cooking more efficient, it will also make it far less stressful. I might add that it also makes it easier to tidy up as you go along, another great skill that professional kitchens have taught me.

BE ADVENTUROUS. Great home cooking is built around the classics, but cooking the same old dishes can soon become a chore. The secret is to not let them go stale. Make sure you keep your cooking exciting by tweaking and adapting it. Over the past 20 years I've really noticed a big change in people's attitudes to what they will and won't eat. People are much more adventurous these days. They love trying new flavours, new ingredients and new cooking techniques, so take inspiration from around the world. Try your hand at Asian noodles or Mexican tacos, make some spicy Middle Eastern meatballs. Even a classic like roast beef and Yorkshire pudding can be given the occasional makeover. It will make a great change for you and your family and give you all renewed enthusiasm.

BE BOLD. One thing cooking has to do is to stand up and be noticed. It doesn't matter if a dish is light and delicate or full-on and gutsy, the flavours should be distinct and clear. You don't want wishy-washy. And that means getting the maximum from your ingredients. The two things I notice home cooks don't use confidently enough are heat and seasoning. Get your pans properly hot before adding your ingredients and don't be afraid to get a good colour on meat and sometimes vegetables, as this will translate into extra flavour. Similarly, season well and early on to bring out the flavour of your ingredients, tasting as you go along.

BE REALISTIC. A little ambition is a good thing, but it's always good to know your limits. Not so much in the complexity of what you make – there's nothing in this book that will be beyond a reasonable cook – but in terms of your menu choice. This is mainly down to good planning. Don't make a meal that requires four dishes to be stir-fried at the last minute, or try making a frozen pudding after you get back from work for dinner that evening. Remember also that practice makes perfect.

BE RELAXED. If you worry that something will go wrong, it probably will, so try not to stress yourself out. Remember, recipes are only there as a guideline and most of the time a little bit too much of this or too little of that is not going to cause a catastrophe. Get the children or your guests involved. Have them chop or stir or lay the table and make the whole process a more social occasion. That way you'll all have a good time – and if something does go wrong, you'll have someone else to blame!

But above all, have fun. Happy cooking!

BREAKFAST AND BRUNCH

CHEFS HAVE A DIFFICULT RELATIONSHIP WITH BREAKFAST.

In truth it's the meal they least like to be on duty for – not just because they're likely to have been at work until 1 a.m. the night before, but also because it involves a lot of last-minute work. With most meals you live or die by your *mise-en-place* (all the preparation you do in the hours before service, getting the vegetables chopped and part cooked, the stocks reduced, the garnishes ready), which leaves you free to concentrate on the main element of the dish. With breakfast, though, it doesn't work like that and there's not much you can do in advance. Inevitably it means more hard work when your guests have already sat down and made their choices – short-order cooking, we call it.

It's easier at home, of course, because you are presumably not giving your friends or family a choice (if you are, you need to stop that right now!), but there is still a danger you'll spend your time chained to the stove, so it's important to plan even a breakfast or brunch carefully and do all you can to make it easy for yourself. The first rule is to choose the right dishes. This will depend in large part on how many you are catering for: pancakes for two is easy; pancakes for 12 is a nightmare. Scrambled eggs and omelettes won't hang around and must be served straight away. Poached eggs, on the other hand, can be cooked in advance and reheated in boiling water.

If your house is like mine, weekday breakfasts are a bit of a write-off. They are a functional business – a quick bowl of cereal, a piece of toast, a hunt for Jack's school tie, and out of the door – but that doesn't mean you can't still have a couple of things on standby. Being a good Scot, I was brought up on porridge, but these days I tend to see that more as a weekend treat, especially my spiced and baked version. Recently, though, I've become a convert to Bircher muesli, a cross between porridge and muesli that makes a fantastically healthy start to the day. You simply soak oats in yoghurt and apple juice, ideally overnight, and top them with toasted nuts, seeds and grated apple the next morning. Another popular dish is home-made granola – a combination of oats, bran and puffed wheat baked with honey and seeds. It will keep for weeks in an airtight jar. By the way, if you are a fan of traditional porridge and need to make it in a hurry, you should either use rolled oats, which have been steamed and flattened into flakes so they cook more quickly, or you can use a trick of my mum's: she soaked more flavoursome pinhead oats in cold water overnight, about 2 parts water to 1 part oats, then cooked them in the usual way the next morning.

For a more leisurely weekend brunch you can get more adventurous. There's the classic repertoire of English dishes, from boiled egg and soldiers,

Eggs Benedict or smoked haddock to the full English, but don't limit yourself to these shores. America has a strong brunch tradition and hash browns and proper home-made baked beans are both brilliant in the morning. You can also go down the spice route to reinvigorate jaded palates. Mexican eggs or even a chilli-flecked Asian fruit salad will perk up your guests in the same way as a spicy Bloody Mary can. And don't forget that French classic, pain perdu, or eggy bread as we always call it. It's brilliant as a savoury accompaniment to baked beans and bacon, but even better dusted with cinnamon and icing sugar and served with stewed apples. After that, you'll be ready to face the day, I promise. Here's my list of breakfast essentials.

BACON
Buy the best you can, traditional dry-cured British out of preference. Ensure it is at room temperature and start with a hot pan. Slices of Parma ham make a quick, super-crispy alternative.

POACHED EGGS
Add a splash of vinegar to a deep pot of simmering water. Crack very fresh eggs into a tea cup, stir the water to create a vortex and then very gently lower into the water. Cook for a couple of minutes, then 'shock' them in iced water, to be reheated in simmering water for 1 minute when needed.

PORRIDGE OATS
Coarser pinhead oats typical of Ireland have a nuttier flavour, but rolled jumbo oats cook more quickly.

SCRAMBLED EGGS
The secrets of soft, rich scrambled eggs are to start with a cold heavy-based pan, only beat the eggs once they're in the pan, and to add cold butter before stirring constantly with a plastic spatula to get right into the corners. If the eggs start sticking, take the pan off the heat for a moment.

HOME-MADE GRANOLA

QUICK BIRCHER MUESLI

SPICED BAKED PORRIDGE

TANGY FRUIT SALAD

CRISPY FILO WITH HONEYED YOGHURT

CINNAMON EGGY BREAD
WITH QUICK STEWED APPLE

EGGS BENEDICT WITH CRISPY
PARMA HAM

BOILED EGGS WITH
ANCHOVY SOLDIERS

SPICED EGG AND SPINACH
BREAKFAST WRAP

FENNEL SAUSAGE FRITTATA

MERGUEZ-SAUSAGE-AND-FONTINA
STUFFED CROISSANTS

SMOKED HADDOCK AND
SPINACH BAKED EGGS

HOME-MADE BAKED BEANS
WITH POTATO CAKES

HASH BROWN BAKED EGGS
WITH CANDIED BACON

BAKED SPICY MEXICAN EGGS

HOME-MADE GRANOLA

SERVES 4

If you've never made your own granola, do try it. It's really healthy and so much cheaper and tastier than the versions you can buy in the shops. You can add any mix of seeds and nuts you like, even a bit of spice such as cinnamon. Goji berries are one of nature's superfoods and are full of vitamins and antioxidants.

200g runny honey
1 vanilla pod, split open and seeds scraped out
300g jumbo rolled oats
100g sugar-free puffed rice
4 tbsp wheat bran or oat bran
100g whole almonds, blanched
75g pumpkin seeds
75g sunflower seeds
50g linseeds
Pinch of sea salt
50g goji berries
50g dried cranberries

1. Preheat the oven to 180°C/Gas 4. Line a shallow baking tin with baking parchment.

2. Put the honey and vanilla seeds in a small pan and heat gently, stirring to combine.

3. Place the oats, puffed rice, bran, almonds and seeds in a mixing bowl. Pour in the honey mixture and stir well. Transfer to the prepared tin, sprinkle with a pinch of salt and bake for 25–30 minutes, stirring now and again to ensure even toasting, until crisp and golden.

4. Once cooked, set aside to cool slightly, then break into small pieces if necessary. Stir in the berries and, once cold, store in an airtight container until wanted.

QUICK BIRCHER MUESLI
SERVES 4

Bircher muesli is like a cross between porridge and regular muesli in which oats are softened, sometimes overnight, in yoghurt, apple juice, milk or a mix of any of the three. It's a great start to the day and one of those simple recipes where you can make it up according to what's to hand – you can add extra seeds, nuts and fruit as you see fit. I always include grated apple for the vitamin C and toast any nuts in a dry pan for extra crunch.

200–250ml yoghurt (flavoured yoghurt,
   e.g. blackberry or vanilla, is great)
4 tbsp apple juice
200g jumbo rolled oats
4 tbsp flaked almonds
½ apple, grated, to garnish (optional)
150g blackberries

1. Whisk the yoghurt and apple juice together in a bowl until well combined, then stir in two-thirds of the oats. If you wish, you can set the mixture aside for up to an hour so the oats soften; otherwise, use it immediately.

2. Once you are ready to serve, toast the almonds in a dry frying pan until golden.

3. Mix the remaining oats. Top the muesli with the blackberries, grated apple (if using) and toasted almonds and serve.

SPICED BAKED PORRIDGE
SERVES 4–6

As a Scot, I have to include porridge, don't I? It is sometimes seen as a bit of an austere breakfast, and made in the traditional way, with just water and salt, it can be. But this is porridge like I never had as a child, enriched with cream, nuts and spices. Cooking it in the oven takes away the pain of having to stir it constantly on the hob, and caramelising the sugar under the grill at the last minute turns it into a kind of healthy crème brulée.

150g jumbo rolled oats
Seeds from 1 vanilla pod
1 tsp ground cinnamon
½ tsp freshly grated nutmeg, plus a little extra to sprinkle
50g whole blanched almonds
50g blanched hazelnuts
75g raisins
1 ripe pear, peeled, cored and chopped into small chunks
500ml milk, plus extra for serving
200ml double cream
2 tbsp demerara sugar

1. Preheat the oven to 180°C/Gas 4.

2. Combine the oats and vanilla seeds in a mixing bowl – use your fingers to rub the seeds through the oats. Add the spices, nuts, raisins and pear and mix well. Stir in the milk and cream, then pour the mixture into a baking dish. Dust with a little extra grated nutmeg.

3. Place in the oven and bake for 30–35 minutes, or until the oats are completely softened and the liquid absorbed.

4. Heat the grill on its highest setting. Sprinkle the top of the porridge with the sugar and place under the grill for 3–4 minutes, or until the sugar has melted and created a crust.

5. Serve warm, with a little extra milk on the side if desired.

TANGY FRUIT SALAD

SERVES 4

I've travelled around the Far East quite a bit over recent years, and as you'd expect, it's opened my eyes to the possibilities of spice. One of the most surprising dishes I came back with is this chilli-spiked fruit salad. It makes a light, refreshing pudding, but I've developed a real taste for it first thing in the morning too. The secret is to make sure your fruit isn't too ripe, so the salad stays crisp and tangy and gives a proper kick-start to your day.

1 small pineapple, peeled, cored and cut into bite-sized pieces

2 crunchy green apples, quartered, cored and cut into bite-sized chunks

2 pears, not too ripe, cored and cut into bite-sized pieces

1 mango, not overly ripe, peeled and cut into bite-sized pieces

½ cucumber, peeled, deseeded and cut into bite-sized chunks

FOR THE DRESSING

1½ tbsp tamarind paste

Zest and juice of 1 lime

2–3 tbsp palm or brown sugar

½–1 red chilli, finely sliced, to taste

3 tbsp skinless unsalted peanuts

Sea salt and freshly ground black pepper

1. First make the dressing. Mix the tamarind paste, lime zest and juice, sugar and chilli, then season with a little salt and pepper. Mix well, taste and adjust the seasoning as necessary.

2. Toast the peanuts in a dry frying pan with a small pinch of salt until golden and toasted. Wrap the nuts in a clean tea towel and run a rolling pin over them to crush them.

3. Mix the crushed peanuts into the dressing. Taste and add a little more sugar and/or salt if needed.

4. Combine the fruits and cucumber in a serving bowl. Add half the dressing and toss well. Taste and add the remaining dressing if needed.

USING TAMARIND

Tamarind's tangy flavour makes it a very useful addition to salads, and it's definitely worth tracking down a jar if you can. Adding a little extra lime juice can sometimes be a good substitute, though you may find the salad will lack a certain fruity sharpness. Tamarind paste can also be used in pad thai and Asian fish dishes, chicken curries and my Sticky Spiced Chicken Wings (page 228).

CRISPY FILO WITH HONEYED YOGHURT

SERVES 4

The combination of pastry, Parmesan, honey and yoghurt may sound strange, but do give these a try. The Greeks often eat feta and filo triangles drizzled with thyme honey and sesame seeds as a snack, so I decided to rework them with Parmesan and added some luxurious thick yoghurt. It's the perfect combination of savoury and sweet and works particularly well for brunch.

50g butter
Small bunch of thyme, leaves only
75g Parmesan or pecorino cheese
4 sheets of filo pastry, each trimmed
   to a large square
Olive oil, for frying
Freshly ground black pepper

TO SERVE
250g Greek or thick yoghurt
2 tbsp runny honey

1. Melt the butter in a small saucepan. Meanwhile, put the thyme leaves in a bowl and mix with a good pinch of pepper.

2. Place a square of filo on a work surface. Brush with a little of the melted butter, sprinkle over a quarter of the thyme leaves and grate over a quarter of the cheese. Brush the edges with butter, fold the square into a triangle and press the edges to seal. Slice the triangle in half, creating two smaller triangles, brush the cut edges with butter and press to seal. Repeat with the remaining pieces of filo until you have 8 triangles in total.

3. Heat a large heavy-based frying pan over a medium heat. Brush the pan with a little oil or any leftover melted butter and fry a few triangles at a time for 1–2 minutes on either side, until crisp and golden. Set aside and keep warm while cooking the remaining triangles.

4. Mix together the yoghurt and honey and serve alongside the crispy filo parcels.

HOW TO HANDLE HONEY
Sticky ingredients, such as honey, treacle and golden syrup, can be a mess to measure out, so rub the spoon first with a neutral oil, like grapeseed. The ingredient will slide off easily.

CINNAMON EGGY BREAD WITH QUICK STEWED APPLE

SERVES 4

Like most families we often have some slightly stale bread knocking around, and this, along with bread and butter pudding, is a great way of using it up. Normally recipes call for the cinnamon and sugar to be sprinkled on only at the end, but I like to add them to the egg mix so that the sugar caramelises slightly as you cook it. A few stewed apples make the perfect accompaniment.

3 free-range eggs, beaten
4 tbsp whole milk
1 tsp ground cinnamon, plus extra for dusting
2 tbsp caster sugar
4 thick slices of slightly stale white bread, halved into triangles
Butter, for frying
Icing sugar, for dusting

FOR THE STEWED APPLE
400g eating apples, e.g. Braeburn, cored and chopped into chunks
2 tpsp caster sugar
25g butter

1. First make the stewed fruit. Begin by melting the caster sugar in a small saucepan or sauté pan, swirl it around in the pan but don't stir it. Once melted, add the apples and butter, cook for 2 minutes before adding a couple of tablespoons of water. Bring to a simmer and cook for 5–8 minutes over a low heat, stirring now and again until the apple begins to collapse and the chunks that remain are tender. Set aside.

2. Meanwhile, put the eggs, milk, cinnamon and sugar into a bowl and mix together. Dip the bread into the egg mixture until saturated on either side.

3. Heat a large frying pan over a medium heat. Add a knob of butter and cook the eggy bread on either side until crisp and golden.

4. Remove and serve with the warm stewed apple dusted with a little icing sugar.

HOW TO VARY THE RECIPE
This works just as well with thinly sliced baguettes and is even more decadent when made with day-old brioche, croissants or panettone.

EGGS BENEDICT WITH CRISPY PARMA HAM

SERVES 4

Supposedly named after a New York stockbroker who ordered poached eggs and hollandaise as a cure for his hangover in the 1890s, this has become the world's most famous brunch dish. It's great with spinach or smoked salmon, but I like it best with crisp Parma ham. Timing is the real challenge here, but the hollandaise will hold in a warm place for 30 minutes or so, and you can always make the poached eggs in advance and reheat them (see the tip below).

Olive oil, for frying
White wine vinegar, for poaching
8 slices of Parma ham
4 free-range eggs
2 English muffins, split in half

FOR THE HOLLANDAISE SAUCE
3 free-range egg yolks
2 tsp tarragon or white wine vinegar
200ml unsalted butter, melted
Lemon juice, to taste
Sea salt and freshly ground black pepper

1. First make the hollandaise. Bring a large pan of water to the boil, then reduce to a simmer. Place a large heatproof bowl over the pan (it should not touch the water) and add the egg yolks. Add the vinegar and whisk vigorously, until the mixture forms a foam, but make sure it doesn't get too hot. If necessary, take it on and off the heat while whisking to prevent this happening. The aim is to achieve a golden, airy foam.

2. Turn the heat off under the pan and whisk in the melted butter a little at a time, until it is all incorporated and you have a texture almost as thick as mayonnaise. Finally, whisk in lemon juice, salt and pepper to taste, plus a little warm water from the pan if the mixture is too thick. Cover and set aside.

3. Heat a frying pan over a medium heat, add a dash of oil and fry the slices of ham until crisp. Remove and drain on kitchen paper.

4. Put the muffin halves in the empty frying pan and toast on both sides until golden and crisp.

5. Meanwhile, bring a saucepan of water to a gentle simmer and add a dash of vinegar. Break an egg into a teacup or ramekin, then whisk the water to create a gentle whirlpool, and tip the egg into the centre of it. Leave to cook for 3 minutes, or until the egg floats to the top and the white is cooked but the yolk still soft. Lift the egg out with a slotted spoon, drain on kitchen paper and season with a pinch of salt. Keep warm while you cook the remaining eggs in the same way.

6. To serve, place each muffin half on a serving plate. Top with a slice of crispy ham and a poached egg. Spoon over the hollandaise sauce, and place the remaining crispy ham on the side.

HOW TO REHEAT POACHED EGGS
If necessary, you can make poached eggs in advance and reheat them by dipping them in simmering water for 30 seconds just before serving.

BOILED EGGS WITH ANCHOVY SOLDIERS

SERVES 2

Who doesn't like boiled eggs and soldiers? It's one of those childhood dishes we tend to forget about but come back to when we have kids of our own. Here I'm turning it on its head by spreading the soldiers with butter and mashed anchovies to make a kind of home-made Gentleman's Relish. It's a great twist on a great classic and guaranteed to make your taste buds stand to attention.

2 free-range eggs

FOR THE ANCHOVY SOLDIERS
5–6 best-quality tinned anchovy fillets in olive oil
Freshly ground black pepper
30–50g butter, softened
4 thin slices of sourdough or pain de
    campagne bread
2 tbsp finely chopped parsley (optional)

1. Drain the anchovies, reserving the oil, and place in a mortar with a pinch of pepper. Pound until smooth, then add the butter and pound again until well mixed. Taste and adjust the seasoning as necessary.

2. Cook the eggs in gently boiling water for 4½ minutes. Remove them as soon as the time is up.

3. Meanwhile, place a heavy-based frying pan over a medium heat and add 1–2 tablespoons of the reserved anchovy oil. Once hot, add the bread and toast it on each side until golden brown.

4. Spread the toast with the anchovy butter, sprinkle with the chopped parsley, if using, and slice into soldiers. Serve alongside the soft-boiled eggs.

HOW TO SOFT BOIL EGGS
The secret to softly boiling eggs is to lower them gently into boiling water on a spoon and tilting it so they don't hit the bottom of the pan. Then count to five, turn the heat down, and cook for four and a half minutes.

SPICED EGG AND
SPINACH BREAKFAST WRAP

SERVES 4

You'll find breakfast wraps like these sold by street vendors all over India and they make a really balanced meal, especially if you are on the go. At home I like to put the curried eggs, spinach mix and bowls of minty yoghurt on the table, leaving everyone to help themselves.

1–2 tsp cumin seeds
1–2 tsp mustard seeds
Olive oil, for frying
1 onion, peeled and finely sliced
Butter, for frying
200g baby spinach, rinsed
1 tsp garam masala
2 tsp ground turmeric
8 free-range eggs
4 parathas or thin naan breads
3 tsp finely shredded mint leaves
6 tbsp natural yoghurt
Sea salt and freshly ground black pepper

1. Toast the cumin and mustard seeds in a lightly oiled pan until aromatic. Add the onion, a knob of butter and a pinch of salt and fry gently over a medium heat for 5–7 minutes, until the onion is tender and dark golden. Add the spinach and cook until wilted. Set aside.

2. Melt another knob of butter in a separate pan with a splash of olive oil. Add the garam masala and 1 teaspoon of the turmeric and cook for a minute or two, until aromatic.

3. Meanwhile, beat the eggs in a bowl. Pour the mixture over the spices, add a knob of butter and gently scramble over a low heat until cooked to your liking. Add another knob of butter to the eggs just before they finish cooking and mix through.

4. Warm the parathas or naan breads according to the packet instructions – usually about 2 minutes in a dry pan.

5. Chop the spinach mixture, discarding any liquid, then fold into the eggs.

6. Add the chopped mint and remaining teaspoon of turmeric to the yoghurt. Season with a pinch of salt and mix well.

7. Divide the egg mixture between the parathas or naan breads. Top with dollops of the yoghurt, then fold over and serve immediately.

FENNEL SAUSAGE FRITTATA

SERVES 4

Sausage and egg, Italian style. The sausage meat is taken out of its casing so it cooks more quickly and allows all the meat flavours to mingle with the onions and fennel. Then you add beaten eggs to make a frittata – essentially an open omelette. Finish it off with melted mozzarella. There's no need to use your best buffalo milk mozzarella for this – any good quality cow's milk mozzarella will do.

Olive oil, for frying
1 onion, peeled and thinly sliced
1 tsp fennel seeds
2–4 Italian fennel sausages (about 350g in total)
8 free-range eggs
Small handful of parsley, finely chopped
50g Parmesan cheese, finely grated
1 ball of good-quality mozzarella cheese, sliced
Sea salt and freshly ground black pepper

1. Heat a non-stick, heavy-based, ovenproof frying pan, add a dash of oil and gently sauté the onion with the fennel seeds and a pinch of salt until soft and lightly caramelising.

2. Meanwhile, remove the sausage meat from the skin.

3. Once the onions are cooked, crumble the sausage meat into the pan, breaking it into small chunks with a wooden spoon. Fry over a medium heat until cooked through and coloured on the outside.

4. Beat the eggs in a bowl and season with salt and pepper. Add the parsley and 25g of the Parmesan. Pour the mixture over the meat, mix well and cook over a medium-low heat for 5–7 minutes, or until the frittata is almost set.

5. Preheat the grill until hot. Arrange the mozzarella over the frittata in a single layer and sprinkle with the remaining Parmesan. Place the pan under the grill for 3–4 minutes, or until the egg is cooked through and the mozzarella melted, bubbling and lightly browned.

6. Set aside to cool slightly, then transfer to a serving board. Cut into wedges to serve.

HOW TO SOFTEN FENNEL SEEDS
Some people worry about fennel seeds being too hard and getting stuck in their teeth. If so, you can always soak them in cold water for 10 minutes and drain them before cooking. This will soften them up nicely.

MERGUEZ-SAUSAGE-AND-FONTINA-STUFFED CROISSANTS

SERVES 4

This is a big, bold and punchy start to the day, a kind of European take on the hot dog, with merguez sausages, garlic and melted cheese, all wrapped up in croissant buns. Merguez are spicy lamb sausages originally from North Africa. When I was living in France I treated myself to them for breakfast at least two or three times a week as they can't fail to wake you up. Fontina is a great cheese for grilling, especially when sliced thinly, but something like Gruyère or Emmenthal would also work well.

Olive oil, for frying
8 merguez sausages, cut into 3cm pieces
2 garlic cloves, peeled and finely sliced
Small handful of chopped parsley
2 tbsp capers, rinsed
4 best-quality croissants
175g Fontina or Port Salut cheese, thinly sliced
Sea salt and freshly ground black pepper

1. Place a frying pan over a medium heat, add a dash of olive oil and fry the sausage slices with a little salt and pepper until cooked through and lightly coloured on the outside. Remove and slice on the diagonal, then place in a bowl.

2. Add the garlic to the pan and fry for 30 seconds, then add the parsley and capers and heat for another 30 seconds. Mix with the sausages.

3. Preheat the grill.

4. Slice the very top off each croissant to create a lid. Fry the cut sides in the hot pan until golden. Gently push down the inside of the croissants to create a hollow, then fill with the sausage mixture. Top with the slices of cheese and season with salt and pepper.

5. Place the filled croissants (without the lids) on a baking sheet and put under the hot grill for 1–2 minutes, until the cheese has melted. Place the lids on top and serve.

HOW TO USE FRESH HERBS IN COOKING
Add the stalks of soft herbs during cooking to impart flavour, and the leaves just before serving to impart maximum fragrance and colour.

SMOKED HADDOCK AND SPINACH BAKED EGGS
SERVES 4–6

The combination of sweetly smoked haddock and spinach is a classic I'd be happy to sit down to at any time of the day, but like kedgeree, it really lends itself to a hearty weekend brunch. Instead of bothering to make a white sauce with milk and flour, I'm using crème fraîche as a quick cheat, cutting the richness with some lovely wholegrain mustard. You could always mix in some crispy bacon pieces or sprinkle over some freshly grated Parmesan before finishing it under the grill if you liked.

Butter, for frying
Olive oil, for frying
300g baby spinach, rinsed
300g undyed, skinless smoked haddock, chopped into chunks
300ml crème fraîche
1 tbsp wholegrain mustard
4 tarragon sprigs, leaves only
6 free-range eggs
4 spring onions, finely sliced
Sea salt and freshly ground black pepper

1. Preheat the oven to 180°C/Gas 4.

2. Place an ovenproof frying pan or shallow casserole dish over a medium heat. Add a knob of butter and a dash of olive oil, then sauté the spinach with a little salt and pepper until wilted. Place the haddock chunks on top of the spinach and steam for 3–4 minutes. Mix the fish into the spinach.

3. Combine the crème fraîche, mustard and tarragon in a bowl, and add a little seasoning to taste. Spoon half the mixture over the spinach and mix. Allow to warm through, then turn off the heat.

4. Break the eggs over the top of the dish. Dot with the remaining crème fraîche and place in the oven for 8–10 minutes, until the whites are cooked through but the yolks still soft.

5. Set aside to cool slightly before sprinkling with spring onions and serving.

HOME-MADE BAKED BEANS WITH POTATO CAKES

SERVES 4

Like every child, I loved tinned baked beans when growing up. They were a real treat and I've never lost the taste for them. Nowadays I like to make my own to get a better balance of sweetness and acidity to suit adult tastes and to add some spice to work against the natural blandness of the beans.

Olive oil, for frying
100g pancetta lardons
1 red chilli, finely sliced
2 garlic cloves, peeled and finely chopped
1 red onion, peeled and finely diced
1 tbsp light muscovado sugar
2 tbsp cider vinegar
Worcestershire sauce, to taste

500ml smooth tomato passata
2 x 400g tins haricot beans, drained
  (or cannellini if you prefer)
Sea salt and freshly ground black pepper

FOR THE POTATO CAKES
500g potatoes, peeled and boiled until tender
50g butter, plus extra for frying
4–5 tbsp plain flour, plus extra for dusting

1. Place an ovenproof saucepan or casserole dish over a medium heat and add a dash of oil. Once hot, add the pancetta, a little pepper and the chilli and fry until cooked through but not crisping. Add the garlic and cook for 2 minutes, then add the onion and cook over a low heat until completely tender, about 5 minutes. Stir in half the sugar, then add the vinegar. Boil for 1 minute, then add Worcestershire sauce to taste.

2. Stir in the passata and season with a good pinch of salt and pepper, the remaining sugar and a couple of shakes of Worcestershire sauce. Bring to a simmer and cook for 4–5 minutes. Add the beans and cook for a further 5–10 minutes, until the sauce has reduced and thickened and the beans are really soft and tender.

3. Meanwhile, make the potato cakes. Mash the boiled potatoes until smooth (or use a potato ricer), add the butter and mix well. Add 4 tablespoons of the flour along with a pinch of salt and pepper and stir well. The aim is to form a dough, so add a little more flour if necessary.

4. Using your hands, roll pieces of the dough into balls just larger than a golf ball. Place them on a lightly floured work surface and flatten them into little cakes about 1cm thick. Chill for 20 minutes.

5. Place a heavy-based frying pan over a medium heat and add a dash of olive oil. When hot, fry the potato cakes on either side (in batches if necessary) until golden and crisping slightly. While cooking, season with a pinch of salt and add a small knob of butter to the pan. Drain the cakes on kitchen paper to remove any excess oil.

6. Taste and adjust the seasoning of the beans as necessary, adding a little more vinegar and/or Worcestershire sauce, as well as salt and pepper. Serve alongside the warm potato cakes.

HOW TO FRY POTATOES WITH BUTTER
Butter gives a lovely rich finish to fried potato, but it burns more easily than oil. For best results, start with oil and then add butter towards the end of your cooking time, using a spoon to baste the potatoes as the butter froths up.

HASH BROWN BAKED EGGS
WITH CANDIED BACON

SERVES 6

The Americans always know a great breakfast, and they love their hash browns. You could make these in a muffin tin to create individual servings, but I like to serve it family-style in one big pan. Make sure you squeeze out all the moisture from the grated potato or else they will boil in the liquid instead of getting that lovely golden crust. The crisp candied bacon completes my tribute to a Stateside brunch.

850g–1kg waxy potatoes, peeled and grated
1 onion, peeled and grated
Olive oil
Cayenne pepper
4 knobs of butter
6 free-range eggs
Sea salt and freshly ground black pepper

FOR THE CANDIED BACON
1 tsp soft brown sugar
Knob of butter
8 rashers of smoked streaky bacon

1. Preheat the oven to 200°C/Gas 6.

2. Place the potatoes and onion in a colander and press to squeeze out any excess moisture. Season with salt and pepper, a drizzle of olive oil and a pinch of cayenne pepper. Mix well, then squeeze again using your hands to get rid of any last traces of moisture.

3. Heat a large ovenproof frying pan over a medium heat. Pour in a dash of olive oil, then add the potato mixture and press down to compact it. Break 2 knobs of butter into small pieces and dot them around the edges of the pan. Continue cooking until the potato is golden and crisp on the bottom.

4. Place a plate over the frying pan, quickly invert both, then slide the potato mixture back into the pan so that the uncooked side is now on the bottom. Break the remaining knobs of butter into pieces, dot them around the edges and continue cooking the potato for 5 minutes, or until the base is golden.

5. Break the eggs on top of the hash brown. Sprinkle with another pinch of cayenne pepper and place into the oven for 6–8 minutes, or until the egg whites are firm but the yolks are still runny.

6. Meanwhile, to cook the bacon, heat a frying pan over a medium heat. Add the sugar, season with a little pepper and add the butter. Once beginning to caramelise, add the bacon and cook for 3–4 minutes on either side, until golden and crisp.

7. To serve, place the hash brown eggs on a warm plate and top with the bacon.

BAKED SPICY MEXICAN EGGS
SERVES 6

Eggs poached or baked in a fiery tomato sauce is a popular breakfast all around the world. There's a famous North African version called shakshuka, which sometimes has artichokes or broad beans in it, but here I'm giving it a more Latin American flavour by adding black beans and cooking it on a base of corn tortillas. Grated cheese and chopped coriander finish it off nicely, but you could always go further and add sliced avocado and sour cream if you like.

Olive oil, for frying and greasing
1 red onion, peeled and diced
1 wide green chilli, e.g. jalapeño, or ordinary green chilli if unavailable, sliced
2 garlic cloves, peeled and finely sliced
1 tsp cumin seeds
1 x 400g tin chopped tomatoes
1 x 400g tin cooked black beans, drained and rinsed
4–6 corn tortillas, halved
6 free-range eggs
50g Cheddar cheese, finely grated
2 pinches of chilli flakes, or to taste
Small handful of coriander, finely chopped
Sea salt and freshly ground black pepper

1. Preheat the oven to 180°C/Gas 4, and heat the grill as well if you have an oven grill function.

2. Place a frying pan over a medium heat and add a glug of olive oil. Add the onion, chilli and garlic with a pinch of salt and pepper and sauté until tender and dark golden, about 6 minutes. Add the cumin and cook until aromatic. Stir in the tomatoes and gently simmer for 5 minutes. Add the beans, heat through for 2 minutes, then set aside.

3. Grease a baking dish with a little oil and sprinkle some seasoning in the bottom of it. Line the dish with the tortillas, overlapping them and raising them slightly above the edge of the dish. Pour in the tomato mixture, then make 6 little wells in it.

4. Break an egg into a cup, then pour it into a well so that the yolk sits neatly in the middle. Repeat with the remaining eggs. Sprinkle over the cheese and chilli flakes and season with salt and pepper.

5. Place the dish on a shelf two-thirds of the way up the oven so that the grill (if on) can colour the cheese. Bake for 8–10 minutes, or until the egg whites are cooked through, the yolks runny and the cheese melted and golden. If you don't have an oven grill, bake for a further 3–4 minutes.

6. Scatter with the coriander before serving.

SOUPS, BREADS AND SANDWICHES

THERE'S A GOOD REASON WHY SOUPS AND SANDWICHES HAVE BECOME THE STAPLE OF A MILLION LUNCHES.

Easy to make and quick to eat, they are a great way of combining different flavours and textures in a single hit. They can also be as grand or as simple as the occasion or your budget demands, from a humble cheese sandwich with a splodge of chutney to a lobster bisque. Made without love or attention, though, they can also be incredibly dreary, as any office worker will attest. There's nothing quite so depressing as a few limp lettuce leaves clamped between slices of cheap bread or a thin watery soup in which you'd struggle to identify a single ingredient.

When you are cooking at home, of course, that need never be an issue and I defy anyone to find anything humdrum about the soups, breads and sandwiches I've put together here. From Welsh rarebit to gazpacho, there's something to keep everyone in the family happy.

As always, the key to success lies in the quality of ingredients you use, so let's start with bread. There's no point in piling your delicious griddled courgettes, ricotta and mint on to a slice of spongy sliced white. Even a chip butty deserves a good-quality white bread. When I was doing my 'stage' with Guy Savoy in Paris, one of my first jobs was making the loaves and rolls. Every night I'd turn out beautiful white, brown, sourdough and cheese breads, and since then I've added other classics such as the Italian focaccia and ciabatta and Middle Eastern flatbreads to my repertoire. Flatbreads are particularly useful as you don't have to wait for them to rise so they're very quick to make and will turn a tub of shop-bought houmous or tzatziki into a decent lunch.

I'm not naïve about expecting you all to start baking your own bread – although you must try my instant Beer Bread on page 91, which can be on the table within 40 minutes – but it is worth buying the best you can and supporting the artisan bakeries that are thankfully having a renaissance. Not only is handcrafted bread healthier for you, with fewer additives and less sugar and salt, but it also tastes so much better. Generally I find sourdough the most versatile. It's made from a starter rather than commercial yeast so has a more complex flavour and, as the name suggests, a slightly sour tang that works really well with cheeses and vegetables. It's more expensive to buy, but I promise you'll never waste any because it can still be used even when several days old. On the first day it's ideal for sandwiches, the next couple of days it can be toasted or used for bruschetta, and by day four it's perfect for making croutons or adding to gazpacho.

Which leads us on to soups. I always think of these as really versatile one-pot wonders. A great way of using up leftover vegetables, you can take them to any level you like, adding things like bacon, mussels and clams for flavour, or noodles, pasta and potatoes for bulk. Gazpacho relies on tomatoes for its liquid but most soups use a stock base. Stock cubes or just water are options here, but it's really not hard to make your own stock, which will give any soup a real boost.

VEGETABLE STOCK

To make a simple vegetable stock, just cover chopped onions, carrots, celery and a halved head of garlic with water, season, and simmer gently for 20 minutes. Then add a glass of wine, a small bundle of herbs – parsley, thyme and tarragon, say – and leave to cool, ideally overnight. Then strain it before using. It will keep in the fridge for five days or freeze for up to six months.

CHICKEN STOCK

Stock made with chicken has a bit more oomph to it, but still lends itself equally to vegetable soups and meaty ones. In the restaurants we'll make two types of chicken stock: a white one with uncooked carcasses for delicate broths and risottos and a brown one with browned vegetables, roasted bones and tomato purée for hearty stews and chunky soups. That's probably more trouble than you'll want to go when cooking for the family. The best compromise is, after a roast dinner, to put the bones and any meat still clinging to them in a large pot with a halved onion, a halved head of garlic and roughly chopped carrots, leeks and a bunch of thyme or parsley. Throw in some peppercorns and just cover it with cold water, then bring it slowly to a simmer and cook for a couple of hours. If you want a clear stock, you'll need to skim the surface of fatty residue regularly as it cooks, but again it's not something to worry about too much. It will still taste great. You can keep stock in the fridge for five days or freeze for up to six months.

CREAMY TOMATO SOUP WITH
SUNDRIED TOMATO PESTO

GAZPACHO

SPICY MEXICAN SOUP

HOME-MADE TORTILLA CHIPS
WITH PICO DE GALLO DIP

SMOKY BACON, SWEETCORN
AND POTATO SOUP

AMERICAN-STYLE CHEESE BISCUITS

STEAMED MUSSELS WITH
CHERRY TOMATOES AND PANCETTA

SAFFRON FLAT BREADS

SPICY CLAM NOODLE SOUP

WELSH RAREBIT

AVOCADO AND BLACK SESAME
SPRINKLE ON SOURDOUGH

PEAR, GOAT'S CHEESE AND
WALNUT TARTINE

PRAWN TOSTADA

COURGETTE AND
RICOTTA BRUSCHETTE

PAN BAGNAT

PLOUGHMAN'S SALAD

BEER BREAD

CHIP BUTTY

CREAMY TOMATO SOUP WITH SUNDRIED TOMATO PESTO

SERVES 4

Few things are as nostalgic as a warming bowl of cream of tomato soup, but, like most foods from childhood, it can be easily improved by employing a few cheffy tricks. Roasting the tomatoes first with garlic, onion and cayenne pepper really helps to intensify their flavour and the charred edges give a lovely smoky quality to the finished soup. Then the sundried tomato pesto at the end is another big hearty flavour booster. Serve with crusty bread or Welsh Rarebit (page 78).

2 red onions, peeled and sliced
2 garlic cloves, peeled and finely sliced
½–1 tsp cayenne pepper, to taste
Olive oil, for drizzling
1.5kg ripe tomatoes, cored and halved
1 tsp caster sugar
1 tsp aged balsamic vinegar
1 litre vegetable or chicken stock
100ml double cream
Sea salt and freshly ground black pepper

FOR THE SUNDRIED TOMATO PESTO
2–3 tbsp pine nuts
75g sundried tomatoes, drained, oil reserved
  and finely chopped
50g Parmesan cheese, grated
Olive oil

HOW TO ENHANCE THE FLAVOUR OF TOMATOES
Adding just a pinch of sugar to cooked tomato dishes or pasta sauces helps to bring out the tomatoes' natural sweetness, especially when the tomatoes aren't as ripe as they might be.

1. Preheat the oven to 180°C/Gas 4.

2. Place a roasting tray on the hob over a medium-high heat. Add the onions, garlic and cayenne pepper, drizzle with enough olive oil to coat, and cook for 3–4 minutes. Add the tomatoes cut side down, season with a pinch of salt, pepper and the sugar, drizzle over the balsamic vinegar and cook over a high heat for 3–4 minutes, until the tomatoes begin to caramelise. Stir well, then transfer to the oven for 20–25 minutes.

3. To make the pesto, start by toasting the pine nuts in a dry frying pan until golden. Put the sundried tomatoes into a mortar and pound with a pestle until completely broken down. Season with a touch of salt, add the pine nuts and continue to pound until you reach a pesto consistency. Stir in the Parmesan, then add the olive oil and enough of the sundried tomato oil to bring the pesto to a spooning consistency (it should provide about 3–4 tablespoons).

4. Place the tray of roasted tomatoes on the hob over a medium heat and pour in the stock. Bring to the boil, then simmer for 4–5 minutes. Add the cream, stir well and continue to simmer for 2–3 minutes.

5. Using a stick blender, blend the soup until almost smooth but still with a couple of chunky bits (use a potato masher for a more rustic texture. Serve warm with dollops of pesto on top.

GAZPACHO

SERVES 4

This refreshing cold Spanish soup has got to be the easiest in the world to make and is perfect served al fresco on a hot summer's day – follow my nifty tip below and you can even take it on a picnic! There's no cooking involved and the only time-consuming thing is waiting for it to chill. The secret is to get the right balance of olive oil, sherry vinegar and seasoning, so do taste as you go along and remember, flavours are more muted when chilled.

1 cucumber, peeled and chopped
1 red pepper, deseeded and chopped
1 green pepper, deseeded and chopped
1kg ripe plum tomatoes, cored and chopped
2 garlic cloves, peeled and crushed
2 spring onions, trimmed and finely chopped
75g stale crusty white bread, chopped
2–2½ tbsp sherry vinegar, or to taste

Small bunch of basil
Extra virgin olive oil
Sea salt and freshly ground black pepper

FOR THE TOASTS (OPTIONAL)
8 thin slices of country-style white bread
Olive oil, for brushing

1. Place the cucumber, peppers, tomatoes, garlic and spring onions in a large bowl. Add the bread, 3–4 basil leaves and season well with salt and pepper. Add the sherry vinegar and a couple of tablespoons of olive oil and mix together with your hands, pressing down to squeeze out the juices. Cover and chill. Leave to marinate for at least 30 mins or overnight.

2. Put the vegetable mixture into a blender and whiz until smooth. Check the consistency. If it is still rather thick and not very rich, add another glug or two of olive oil until you reach a consistency you like. Taste and adjust the seasoning as necessary. You might need a little more vinegar. Cover and chill again, until really cold and you're ready to serve. (At this point, you can freeze some in ice-cube trays, as suggested in the tip below).

3. Meanwhile, make the toasts, if using. Brush the slices of bread generously with olive oil. Place a large griddle pan over a medium heat. Once hot, add the bread and toast on either side until golden and crunchy. Drain on kitchen paper, then season with a little salt and pepper.

4. To serve, stir the gazpacho and taste again as the seasoning may have changed as the soup is now very cold. Adjust as necessary, then serve ice cold with gazpacho ice cubes, sprinkled with the rest of the basil, chopped, an extra drizzle of olive oil and the toasts alongside, if using.

HOW TO KEEP GAZPACHO CHILLED
A clever trick to make sure gazpacho – or any cold soup – stays well chilled is to freeze small amounts in an ice cube tray and add these to the soup just before serving (or, if you're going to a picnic, just before setting out). The soup will be deliciously chilled without being watered down as it would by ordinary ice cubes.

SPICY MEXICAN SOUP

SERVES 4

Chillies come in all shapes, sizes and strengths and are used throughout the world, but if there's one country that has turned cooking them into an art form, it's Mexico. It's not all about blowing your head off with their heat: the Mexicans are masters at building layer upon layer of flavour. The chipotle is a smoked and dried jalapeño chilli, which lends serious heat to this rustic soup. Great served with pico de gallo dip and my home-made tortilla chips (see page 66).

Olive oil, for frying
1 red onion, peeled and diced
2 tsp cumin seeds, dry-toasted
1 tsp dried oregano
2 garlic cloves, peeled and chopped
2–4 dried chipotle chillies, finely chopped, or 1 tbsp chipotle chilli paste, to taste
1 tbsp tomato purée
1 x 400g tin chopped tomatoes
1 x 400g tin cooked kidney beans, drained and rinsed
1 tsp sugar
500–750ml vegetable or chicken stock
100g Lancashire cheese, crumbled
1 ripe avocado, peeled and chopped
½ bunch of coriander, roughly chopped
Sea salt and freshly ground black pepper

1. Place a large heavy-based sauté pan or hob-proof casserole dish over a medium heat and add a dash of olive oil. Once hot, fry the onion with a pinch of salt and pepper until softened. Add the cumin seeds and oregano and cook for a further 2 minutes, or until the seeds become aromatic.

2. Add the garlic and dried chillies (if using), cook for 2 minutes, then add the tomato purée. (If using chipotle paste, add it when you add the purée.) Stir over the heat for a minute or two, then add the tomatoes and kidney beans along with the sugar. Stir and bring to a simmer, then add 500ml of the stock. Bring to the boil, reduce the heat and gently simmer for 10–15 minutes, until thickened slightly and flavoursome. Add a little extra stock if it thickens too much.

3. Pour the soup into warmed serving bowls and sprinkle with the cheese, avocado and coriander.

HOW TO MAXIMISE HEAT FROM CHILLIES
The longer dried chillies are cooked, the hotter they will become, as they swell and release their heat. The Mexicans like to temper this with a natural fire blanket of avocado and a creamy hard cheese similar to Lancashire.

HOME-MADE TORTILLA CHIPS WITH PICO DE GALLO DIP

SERVES 4

Pico de gallo is a Mexican salsa made of tomato, onion and chilli. It is traditionally made with the red serrano chilli, but I prefer the easier-to-find green jalapeño. Remember, the hottest part of any chilli is the membrane that holds the seeds, so scrape this out before chopping if you are sensitive to heat. This is delicious alongside the Spicy Mexican Soup (page 64).

6 large wheat tortilla wraps
Olive oil, for brushing
Smoked paprika
Sea salt and freshly ground black pepper

FOR THE PICO DE GALLO DIP
3 ripe tomatoes, finely diced
½ red onion, peeled and finely diced
1–2 fresh jalapeño chillies, or 1–2 tbsp bottled
  jalapeños in brine, chopped
Small bunch of coriander, finely chopped
Juice of ½ lime

1. Preheat the oven to 180°C/Gas 4. Meanwhile, make the dip. Mix the tomatoes and onion together in a bowl and season with salt and pepper. Add the chillies, coriander and lime juice and mix well. Taste and adjust the seasoning as necessary, then leave to stand for 15 minutes.

2. Brush the tortilla wraps with olive oil on both sides, sprinkle each side with smoked paprika and a pinch of salt, then slice into triangles. Place on one or more baking sheets in a single layer and bake for 3–4 minutes, until golden and crisp. Set aside to cool.

3. Serve the dip with the tortilla chips alongside.

HOW TO HANDLE CHILLIES
When you've been chopping chillies, rub your hands with olive oil before washing them. The oil helps dissolve the capsaicin, the source of the chilli's heat, which is more soluble in oil than in water, and it will then rinse away easily.

SMOKY BACON, SWEETCORN AND POTATO SOUP

SERVES 4–6

You can make a tasty and nourishing soup out of the humblest ingredients, as this sweetcorn chowder shows. I like to make it with a combination of creamed corn and whole kernels so it has good depth of flavour but keeps its chunky texture. You can always purée it if you prefer, adding the bits of bacon at the end. Serve with my American-style Cheese Biscuits (page 70) to make it a meal in its own right.

Olive oil, for frying
1 onion, peeled and diced
4 rashers of smoked streaky bacon, chopped into small pieces
2 bay leaves
2 potatoes, peeled and diced into 1cm cubes
1 leek, trimmed and finely chopped
1 x 375g tin creamed corn
1 x 200g tin sweetcorn, drained
750ml chicken or vegetable stock
500ml whole milk
Sea salt and freshly ground black pepper

1. Place a large saucepan or hob-proof casserole dish over a medium heat. Add a dash of oil and fry the onion until softened. Add the bacon and continue to cook until lightly coloured. Stir in the bay leaves.

2. Add the potatoes and leek and cook for 5–7 minutes, until the leek is soft.

3. Stir in the creamed corn and sweetcorn, then pour in the stock and milk. Bring to a gentle simmer and cook for 15 minutes, or until the potatoes are completely soft and the flavour well developed. Taste and adjust the seasoning as necessary. Serve in warm bowls.

AMERICAN-STYLE
CHEESE BISCUITS
MAKES 12

These are a cross between a scone and a biscuit. They look like scones before they go in the oven and start to rise like them, but because they are rich with cream, they flatten slightly during cooking and end up with a delicious chewy, crumbly texture and an intense cheesy taste. They are incredibly more-ish – it's almost impossible not to have more than one. Try these with my Smoky Bacon, Sweetcorn and Potato Soup (page 68).

375g plain flour
1½ tbsp baking powder
2 tsp sea salt flakes
Freshly ground black pepper
100g extra mature Cheddar cheese, grated
600ml double cream
30g butter, melted

1. Preheat the oven to 160°C/Gas 3. Line one or more baking sheets with baking parchment.

2. Sift the flour and baking powder into a large bowl, add the salt and a good grinding of pepper, then stir in the cheese. Make a well in the middle, pour in the cream and stir gently with a wooden spoon, mixing until a dough forms.

3. Turn the dough on to a lightly floured work surface and knead gently for a few seconds. Don't overwork it or the dough will not rise.

4. With a lightly floured rolling pin and work surface, roll out the dough to a thickness of 2cm. Using a 6cm cutter, stamp out 12 circles, dipping the cutter in flour between each cut so that the dough is easier to remove.

5. Place the circles on the prepared baking sheet(s), spacing them at least 2cm apart as they will spread during cooking. Set aside to rest on the tray for 10 minutes before baking.

6. Brush the top of the biscuits with melted butter and bake for about 30 minutes, until golden brown and well risen. Transfer to a wire rack and serve warm or cold.

HOW TO WORK BISCUIT DOUGH
It's important not to overwork the dough, either when mixing it or kneading it, or the biscuits will end up tough. Dipping your cutter in flour first will make it easier to release the rounds of dough.

STEAMED MUSSELS
WITH CHERRY TOMATOES
AND PANCETTA

SERVES 4

Not really a soup as such, but still a perfect one-bowl meal. You can add so many twists to the classic French moules marinière. Traditionally it's made with white wine, but I've seen it with Guinness, cider... you name it. I'm using sherry here, which gives it more of a Spanish feel. Throw in some bacon, a few tomatoes, some fresh oregano, and you've got a delicious light lunch or serve with Saffron Flat Breads (page 73) for a more substantial meal. Photograph overleaf.

Olive oil, for frying
100g pancetta, chopped into lardons or chunks
1 red chilli, sliced
2 garlic cloves, peeled and bashed
300g cherry tomatoes
1.5kg mussels, scrubbed clean, beards removed
   (discard any that do not shut tight when tapped)
250ml dry sherry
Small handful of oregano, finely chopped

1. Place a large heavy-based casserole dish or saucepan over a medium heat and add a dash of oil. Once hot, fry the pancetta until cooked through and crisping.

2. Add the chilli and garlic and cook for a further 2 minutes. Add the tomatoes and cook for 3–4 minutes, or until they are warmed through and beginning to collapse slightly and blister.

3. Tip in the mussels and oregano. Add the sherry, cover with a lid and cook for 4–5 minutes, or until all the mussels have opened. Discard any that remain shut.

4. Transfer to a serving bowl and serve immediately.

USING MUSSELS
The rule when cooking mussels is to discard any that aren't tightly shut before cooking and then to throw out any that don't open during cooking.

SAFFRON FLAT BREADS

SERVES 4

I've included these simple flat breads to go with the Spanish-inspired Steamed Mussels with Cherry Tomatoes and Pancetta (page 72) because saffron is one of Spain's most famous crops and goes well with sherry. But truth be told, they make a great lunch in their own right with maybe a tub of houmous or tzatziki. As their name suggests, you don't need to wait for the dough to rise, which means that flat breads are a doddle to make. Photograph overleaf.

2 generous pinches of saffron strands
250g plain flour, plus extra for dusting
3 tbsp olive oil
Sea salt and freshly ground black pepper

1. Put the saffron in a bowl and add just enough hot water to cover it. Leave to soak for 10 minutes.

2. Place the flour in a mixing bowl with the olive oil and a couple of pinches of salt and pepper. Pour in the saffron and its soaking liquid, add another 100ml of warm water and mix thoroughly until you have a lump-free dough. If the mixture is too sticky, add a little more flour; if it's too dry, add a tiny drop more warm water.

3. Knead the dough for 2–3 minutes on a floured work surface until smooth and elastic. Place in a clean bowl, cover and leave to rest at room temperature for 15–20 minutes.

4. When ready, divide the dough into 4 equal pieces. Place on a floured work surface and use a floured rolling pin to roll each piece into a circle about 2–3mm thick.

5. Place a large, non-stick, heavy-based frying pan over a medium heat. When hot, cook the flat breads one at a time for 1–2 minutes on either side, until golden. Keep warm whilst you cook the remaining flat breads. Serve warm, cut into pieces.

STEAMED MUSSELS WITH CHERRY TOMATOES AND PANCETTA
(RECIPE PAGE 72)

SAFFRON FLAT BREADS (RECIPE PAGE 73)

SPICY CLAM NOODLE SOUP

SERVES 4

You'll see people eating these huge bowls of noodle soup all over Asia. It's such a simple dish, which you can vary endlessly with different vegetables, noodles, dumplings, fish or meat. What I love most is it's a complete meal in itself – carbs, protein and veg, all in one big bowl of happiness.

1.5 litres fish stock or light chicken stock
3cm piece of fresh root galangal, sliced
1–2 banana shallots, peeled and very finely sliced
3cm piece of fresh root ginger, peeled and sliced
1–2 red chillies, depending on heat, sliced
4 kaffir lime leaves, torn
Bunch of coriander, stalks finely chopped, leaves roughly chopped
2–4 lemongrass stalks, to taste
300g rice noodles, e.g. Thai rice sticks
1kg fresh clams, cleaned and well rinsed
150g beansprouts
Pinch of sugar
Fish sauce (available ready-made from supermarkets)
Juice of 1 lime

1. Place the stock in a large saucepan. Add the galangal, shallots, ginger, chilli, lime leaves and the finely chopped coriander stalks. Bash the lemongrass with the back of your knife to bruise it, chop each stalk into 4 pieces and add to the stock. Bring to a simmer and cook gently for 10 minutes, until aromatic and well flavoured.

2. Cook or soak the noodles according to the packet instructions.

3. Meanwhile, sort through the clams, discarding any that do not shut tightly when tapped.

4. Once ready to serve, add the clams to the soup broth and bring to the boil. Simmer for 3–5 minutes, or until all the clams have opened up. Discard any that remain closed.

5. Drain the noodles and divide between warmed serving bowls. Add the beansprouts. Taste the soup and add a pinch of sugar and dash of fish sauce as necessary (the amount depends on how salty the clams are). Stir in half the lime juice, taste and add more if you wish.

6. Pour the soup over each bowl of noodles, garnish with the coriander leaves and serve immediately.

HOW TO PEEL ROOT GINGER
The easiest way to peel ginger, getting neatly around all those knobbly bits, is to use a teaspoon rather than a knife.

WELSH RAREBIT

SERVES 4

Welsh rarebit is so much more than just fancy cheese on toast. When it's cold and wet outside it hits the spot in a way that few other comfort foods can. Maybe it's the beer, maybe it's the mustard and Worcestershire sauce, but either way, it's a great hearty lunch, especially when it's paired with the Creamy Tomato Soup With Sundried Tomato Pesto on page 60.

50g butter
3 tbsp flour
150ml beer or strong ale
1 heaped tsp Dijon mustard
Worcestershire sauce, to taste
200g best-quality Cheddar cheese,
    e.g. Montgomery
4 large slices of rustic country bread
Sea salt and freshly ground black pepper

1. Preheat the grill until medium hot.

2. Melt the butter in a small saucepan. Add the flour and mix well to make a roux. Heat for 2–3 minutes, stirring constantly, until the rawness is cooked out.

3. Slowly pour in the beer, stirring until well combined. Remove from the heat, add the mustard and Worcestershire sauce and mix again. Add three-quarters of the cheese and beat until it has completely melted. Set aside to cool.

4. Meanwhile, toast the slices of bread on either side until golden. Place them on a baking sheet and spoon the cheese mixture over each slice, so they are completely covered. Sprinkle with the remaining cheese and a few drops of Worcestershire sauce on top. Place the rarebits under the hot grill until dark golden and bubbling. Allow to cool slightly, then serve.

AVOCADO AND BLACK SESAME SPRINKLE ON SOURDOUGH

SERVES 4

It doesn't take much to turn an avocado into a simple meal. As a treat when I was young I would occasionally have half an avocado with its hollow filled with Worcestershire sauce. I thought that was the height of sophistication, but avocado with chilli and sesame seeds is even better. It's great as a healthy, light breakfast or you could top it off with a sardine fillet if you wanted to make this even more substantial.

4 large slices of sourdough bread
Zest and juice of 1 lemon
2–4 pinches of chilli flakes, or to taste
1 tbsp black sesame seeds
2 ripe avocados
Sea salt and freshly ground black pepper
Olive oil

1. Season the bread with salt and pepper and drizzle with a little oil. Toast or griddle the bread until golden brown.

2. Meanwhile, mix together the lemon zest, chilli flakes and sesame seeds with a pinch of salt and pepper.

3. Quarter the avocados, removing the stone and peeling off the skin. Slice each quarter lengthways, leaving the slices joined at the top. Fan out each quarter and place 2 on a piece of toast, pushing down to make them stick.

4. Squeeze a little lemon juice over the avocado, then sprinkle with the sesame seed mixture. Eat immediately while still warm.

HOW TO STONE AN AVOCADO
Cut the avocado in half lengthways and then place the half with the stone still attached on a work surface. Chop into the stone with a sharp knife and you should be able to ease it out.

PEAR, GOAT'S CHEESE
AND WALNUT TARTINE
SERVES 4

I spent three years working in Paris and it opened
my eyes to how exciting an open sandwich could
be. While friends back home were tucking into
jam sandwiches for their tea, I was revelling in
wonderful tartines like this. Don't even think of
spoiling your lovely goat's cheese or ripe pears
with cheap bread. Now is the time to splash out
on a lovely sourdough or crusty French baguette.
This lovely tartine is a perfect accompaniment to
my Tuna Niçoise Salad (page 116).

1 baguette or small sourdough loaf
Olive oil, for griddling
2 pears, e.g. Williams, quartered, cored and
 thinly sliced
150g French goat's cheese, e.g. crottin, soft
 or ripe, cut into the same number of slices as
 the pears
Freshly ground black pepper
4 tbsp walnuts, roughly chopped or crumbled

1. Preheat the grill on its highest setting.

2. If using a baguette, slice it in half across the middle
and trim off the very ends. Slice each half into
4 pieces to give 8 in total. If using a sourdough loaf,
cut it into 8 slices about 2cm thick.

3. Place a griddle pan over a high heat. When hot,
drizzle with a little oil and lower the heat. Add the
bread and toast on either side until lightly crisp
and golden.

4. Transfer the toasts to a baking sheet. Arrange the
pear and cheese slices alternately on each one.
Season with pepper and sprinkle with the walnuts.
Grill for 1–2 minutes, until the cheese has melted.
Serve immediately.

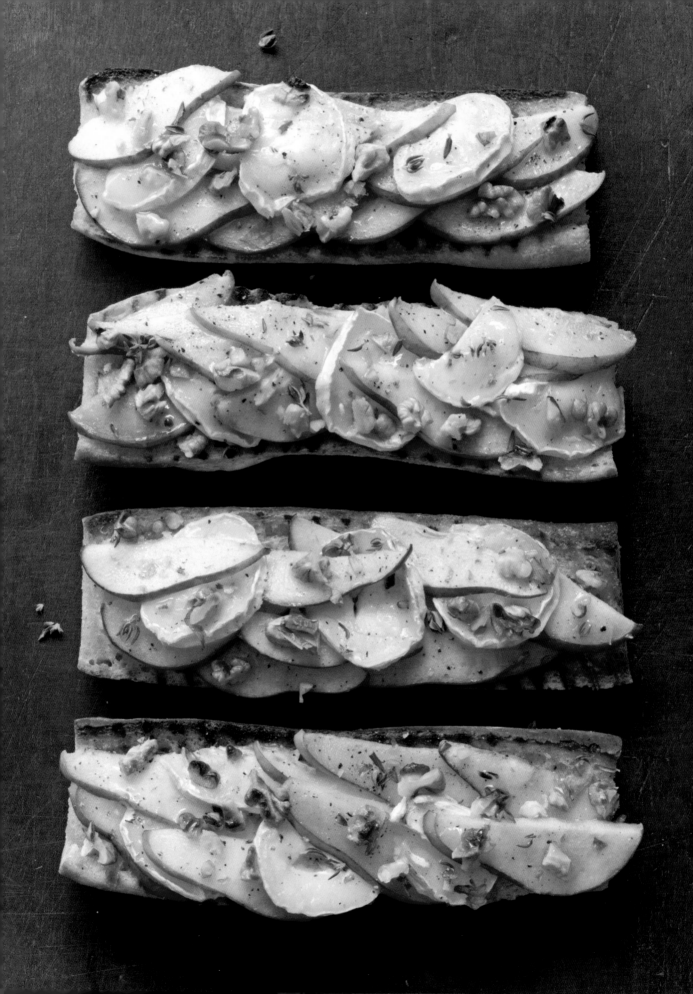

PRAWN TOSTADA

SERVES 4

These are all about the contrast of textures: succulent prawns and soft, ripe avocado mixed with crisp radishes and served on a lovely crunchy tortilla base. In Mexico, the tortillas are normally deep fried in oil, but I find toasting them in a dry pan works just as well and makes them much healthier. You can also make the tostadas in the oven. Brush them with a little oil, if you like, and bake them for 10–15 minutes at 180ºC/Gas 4.

400g raw king prawns, peeled and deveined
2 garlic cloves, peeled and finely sliced
1 tsp chilli flakes, or to taste
Olive oil
1–2 ripe avocados, depending on size, peeled, stoned and diced
4 spring onions, trimmed and finely chopped
1 red chilli, seeded and finely sliced
8–12 radishes, trimmed and quartered
8–12 cherry tomatoes, halved
Juice of 1 lime
2 baby gem lettuces, shredded
Small bunch of coriander, chopped
4 corn flour tortillas
Sea salt and freshly ground black pepper

1. Put the prawns, garlic and chilli flakes into a bowl with a pinch of salt and pepper and a little drizzle of olive oil. Mix well, then set aside.

2. Put the avocados, spring onions, chilli, radishes and tomatoes into another bowl and mix together. Taste and season with salt, pepper and half the lime juice. Mix well, stir in the lettuce, then the coriander and set aside.

3. Heat a dash of oil in a heavy-based frying pan. Extract the prawns from their marinade and fry them for about 2 minutes on each side, until just cooked through. Sprinkle with the remaining lime juice and stir.

4. Toast the tortillas in a dry pan until nicely coloured and beginning to crisp up.

5. Divide the salad equally between the toasted tortillas, top with the cooked prawns and serve.

HOW TO PREPARE PRAWNS
First, twist off the head, then peel off all the shell and pull off the tail. With the tip of a sharp knife, score the prawn along the back and lift out the black vein. Rinse the prepared prawns before using.

COURGETTE AND RICOTTA BRUSCHETTE

SERVES 4

An easy vegetarian lunch or starter for a summer dinner party: freshly griddled courgettes on top of creamy ricotta cheese and crunchy ciabatta toast. Utterly simple but utterly delicious.

2 courgettes, cut into diagonal slices 5mm thick
Olive oil, for drizzling
8 thick slices of ciabatta bread
4 mint sprigs, leaves only
200g ricotta cheese
Sea salt and freshly ground black pepper

1. Place the courgettes in a bowl with a glug of olive oil and a couple of pinches of salt and pepper and toss to coat.

2. Heat a griddle pan until really hot, add the courgette slices in a single layer (they'll need to be done in batches) and cook until golden and striped on both sides. Transfer to a plate and set aside.

3. Drizzle a little olive oil on either side of the bread slices, and griddle until golden and toasted on both sides.

4. Meanwhile, chop the mint leaves and place in a bowl with the ricotta (reserving a little to use as a garnish) and a pinch of salt and pepper. Mix well, then taste and adjust the seasoning as necessary.

5. Spread the toast with the ricotta mixture, top with slices of courgette and garnish with mint leaves. Serve immediately.

USING RICOTTA
Ricotta is a great ingredient to keep in the fridge as it works for both savoury and sweet dishes. Try mixing it with cooked spinach and nutmeg and spreading it over puff pastry for a simple pizza, or add sugar and lemon zest and spoon it over raspberries for a quick dessert.

PAN BAGNAT

SERVES 4–6

This Provençal classic – essentially a salade Niçoise in a sandwich – is the French equivalent of our Cornish pasty, supposedly a handy way for labourers to transport a healthy lunch. My version isn't entirely authentic. I've added mozzarella, which no self-respecting Frenchman would do, and have made it as one giant sandwich, but when you cut it open you'll see that it contains all that is good about summer.

2 courgettes, thinly sliced
Olive oil
1 large round white rustic loaf, e.g. pain
   de campagne or sourdough
12 slices of ham, e.g. Parma ham
2 roasted red peppers (bottled peppers, drained,
   are fine)
2 balls of buffalo mozzarella, drained and torn into
   bite-sized pieces
200g sunblush or sundried tomatoes, drained
Sea salt and freshly ground black pepper

FOR THE TAPENADE
200g pitted black olives, finely chopped
1 garlic clove, peeled and crushed
1 tbsp capers, drained and chopped
4 anchovy fillets, chopped
2 tsp red wine vinegar
1 tbsp extra virgin olive oil

1. First make the tapenade. Put the olives, garlic, capers, anchovies, olive oil and vinegar in a blender and mix well. (If making this by hand rather than in a food processor, you can combine everything in a mortar.) Taste and adjust the seasoning as necessary. Set aside.

2. Meanwhile, place a griddle pan over a high heat. Once hot, toss the courgette slices in a little olive oil, salt and pepper and griddle them on either side until golden and charred. Set aside to cool slightly.

3. Slice a 'lid' off the loaf about 4cm from the top. Scoop out the doughy middle of the bread, leaving a 2.5cm shell. (The bread removed can be turned into crumbs and frozen for later use.) Spread the inside of the loaf with the tapenade. Store any extra tapenade in an airtight container in the fridge for up to a week.

4. Line the insides of the loaf with the slices of Parma ham overlapping them and leaving an inch or so overhanging at the top. Arrange the remaining ingredients inside the prepared shell, using a quarter of them at a time, so that you have 4 layers of each: for example, use a quarter of the peppers, followed by a quarter of the mozzarella and so on until you reach the top of the loaf. Fold the overhanging edges of Parma ham back to the top of the filling to enclose it. Place the lid firmly on top and wrap tightly in cling film. Chill for 2 hours, or overnight if not using straight away.

5. To serve, unwrap the loaf and slice into wedges or thick slices.

PLOUGHMAN'S SALAD
SERVES 4

The ploughman's has been a mainstay of pub menus since the Fifties – quite rightly because it was an instant classic the moment it was dreamt up by the Cheese Marketing Board. Given the choice of ham, Cheddar or Stilton I can never make up my mind, so I thought why not combine all three and top it off with my instant Beer Bread loaves (page 91). Photograph overleaf.

100g watercress, excess stalks cut off
1 romaine lettuce, roughly sliced
1 English eating apple, quartered, cored and cut into small chunks
3 celery sticks, trimmed and finely sliced
8–10 radishes, trimmed and sliced
6–8 slices of cooked ham, torn into pieces
100g best-quality Cheddar cheese, e.g. Montgomery, cut into strips with a vegetable peeler
100g best-quality Stilton, e.g. Colston Basset, cut into small cubes

FOR THE QUICK PICKLED ONION
1 red onion, peeled and very thinly sliced into rings
½ tbsp golden caster sugar
4 cloves
2–3 tbsp red wine vinegar
Pinch of sea salt

FOR THE DRESSING
½–1 tsp English mustard, to taste
1 tsp runny honey
2–3 tbsp white wine vinegar
4 tbsp olive oil
Sea salt and freshly ground black pepper

1. First make the pickled onion. Put the onion into a bowl and sprinkle with the sugar, cloves, vinegar and a pinch of salt. Toss well to mix, place a saucer or layer of cling film over the onions and weigh down with a can of jar. Leave while you prepare the salad, or for up to an hour.

2. To make the dressing, put the mustard, honey, vinegar and oil into a bowl, add a pinch of salt and pepper and stir to combine. Taste and adjust the seasoning as necessary. Set aside.

3. Place the watercress, lettuce, apple, celery and radishes in a bowl and mix together. Mix the dressing again, pour it over the salad and toss to ensure everything is lightly coated.

4. Dot pieces of the ham and cheeses over the top. Drain the pickled onion and dot this over too. Toss lightly and serve.

HOW TO LIGHTEN DRESSINGS
If you find your dressing is a bit heavy (which can sometimes be the case with olive oil vinaigrettes), add some groundnut oil or a touch of water to loosen, or lighten it.

BEER BREAD

MAKES 8 MINI LOAVES

People don't believe me when I say you can have home-made bread on the table within 40 minutes, but here's the proof. These mini loaves are a kind of English take on Irish soda bread, using the fizziness of the beer as the raising agent. The batter will appear unusually runny for a bread mix but don't worry, they'll come out fine. More than that, they'll be delicious. Try them with my Ploughman's Salad (page 90). Photograph overleaf.

Butter, for greasing
175g self-raising flour, plus extra for dusting
75g wholemeal self-raising flour
½ tbsp flaked sea salt, e.g. Maldon
250ml beer or lager
1–2 tbsp milk

1. Preheat the oven to 180°C/Gas 4. Grease 8 mini loaf tins (4.5 x 7.5 x 3cm), then dust with flour and shake out any excess.

2. Sift the flours into a mixing bowl and add the salt. Pour in the beer, mixing as you do so, until the mixture is free of lumps. The batter will appear unusually runny for a bread mix.

3. Divide the batter between the prepared tins, filling them three-quarters full, place on a baking sheet and bake for 30 minutes. Brush the tops with a little milk and a light dusting of flour (to help the tops colour nicely) and bake for a further 5 minutes, or until a skewer inserted into the middle of the loaf comes out clean, and the bottom sounds hollow when tapped.

4. Remove the loaves from the tins and cool on a wire rack. They can be eaten warm or cold, and will keep for a couple of days in an airtight container.

BEER BREAD (RECIPE PAGE 91)

PLOUGHMAN'S SALAD (RECIPE PAGE 90)

CHIP BUTTY

SERVES 4

Ah, this takes me back. I used to love chip butties
– all those different-sized chips smothered with
tomato ketchup and sandwiched between two slices
of squishy white bread. The only concession I've
made to modernity is to roast the chips instead of
deep-frying them, and to season them with smoked
paprika. I think even my nine-year-old self would
have approved.

Groundnut oil, for roasting
750g potatoes, e.g. Desirée, peeled
1 tsp smoked paprika
8 slices of crusty white bread
Butter (optional)
Tomato ketchup (optional)
Sea salt and freshly ground black pepper

1. Preheat the oven to 220°C/Gas 7. Oil a baking tray.

2. Chop the potatoes into batons 1cm thick. Blanch
in boiling salted water for 3–4 minutes, then drain
and place on the prepared tray in a single layer.

3. Drizzle the potatoes with oil and toss to coat evenly.
Season with the smoked paprika and some salt and
pepper. Bake for 15–20 minutes, turning now and
again to ensure even cooking, until golden and crisp.

4. Spread the slices of bread with butter, or rub them
in the remnants of paprika oil in the baking tray.
Sandwich the chips inside bread, adding ketchup
if you wish, then slice in half and serve immediately.

HOW TO CHOOSE POTATOES
Potatoes come in three types: floury, waxy and
all-rounders. Floury potatoes such as King Edwards
are best for mashing, frying and roasting. Waxy
potatoes like Charlottes are perfect for boiling and
in salads. And finally there are all-rounders such
as Desirée, which make great oven chips.

SALAD FOR LUNCH

WHEN I FIRST STARTED COOKING, ALL THE HIGH-END RESTAURANTS SERVED RICH, FRENCH FOOD WITH LOTS OF HEAVY SAUCES FULL OF CREAM AND BUTTER.

You'd see customers come in for four- or five-course lunches and wonder how on earth they were going to stay awake to do an afternoon's work. Luckily the fashion since then has been to make dishes much lighter and fresher by using lots of raw ingredients, herbs and citrus flavours. That's something we try to stick to at home too. Apart from Sundays, when we'll make it the main meal of the day, lunch isn't the time to go overboard. You want something tasty and satisfying that will give you energy without weighing you down.

People sometimes talk disparagingly about 'ladies who lunch' – those glamorous, skinny-as-a-beanpole women who push a starter-size portion of food around their plates and barely touch a thing. I think it's sad when someone clearly doesn't have an appetite for good food, but I have to admit I think they've got the right idea when it comes to what they are ordering: lots of salads, lots of vegetables, lots of simply grilled fish or white meat. That's the kind of thing I like to make for lunch at home too. Although I dare say my portion sizes are bigger than theirs.

It's taken the British a long time to get the hang of salads. I remember when I made my first series of *Kitchen Nightmares* I had a salad in one restaurant where they served up a huge bowl layered with iceberg lettuce, unripe tomatoes, thickly cut cucumber and a carpet of cress on top. No seasoning, no dressing, no nothing. Why didn't it surprise me when I heard the chef later refer to salad as 'rabbit food'? But with a bit of imagination, salads can be wonderful things, especially when you take in influences from around the world and pair unusual ingredients together. We're all familiar nowadays with classic combinations like Caesar salad or Salade Niçoise, but feta and watermelon, or carrot, cumin and orange work just as well together. Or you can take things in a South American direction with raw mackerel ceviche with fennel and grapefruit. Japan is also a great source of inspiration. The Japanese have always favoured light, healthy foods and sticky teriyaki salmon with a simple soba noodle salad makes an ideal lunch. Here are some simple tips for a perfect light lunch.

A CLASSIC VINAIGRETTE

A classic vinaigrette is 3 parts oil to 1 part vinegar. I tend to use a mix of olive oil and groundnut oil so it ends up less rich and gloopy. Alternatively, I might let the vinaigrette down with a little water to lighten it. You can flavour your vinaigrette with anything you like: garlic, wholegrain mustard, herbs and different-flavoured oils such as walnut are the most obvious.

A SIMPLE ASIAN DRESSING

I love this dressing with grilled chicken, salmon or prawns. Mix equal parts of honey and soy sauce with a splash of rice vinegar and whisk in sesame and groundnut oil until you have a dressing the consistency of anything between vinaigrette and mayonnaise.

HOW TO DRESS A SALAD

The two keys are not to use too much vinaigrette and not to dress your leaves until the last minute or else they will wilt. I find using your hands is the best way to gently coat them. A neat trick I learnt in France is to make your vinaigrette in the salad bowl, starting by smearing a cut garlic bulb all around the bowl and using a whisk to combine the vinegar, seasoning and oil. Then you place your salad servers crossed over in the bowl to create a kind of platform to rest the salad leaves on, clear of the vinaigrette. Then when you are ready, you give it a quick toss and you are good to go.

GRILLING

This is a great, healthy way of cooking meat and fish as the fat drains away as you cook. If you want to get those professional-looking charred grill marks, you'll need a ridged grill pan. Get the pan really hot before you start cooking, then brush the food with oil and press down on to the ridges. Don't be tempted to move the food around as it cooks. This is especially true of fish. Once it is cooked, it will release itself from the pan, but if you try to move it too early, it may stick and tear.

ANCHOVY DIP WITH CRUDITÉS

BURRATA WITH QUICK BALSAMIC
FIG JAM AND CROSTINI

BIG CAESAR SALAD

HALLOUMI, COURGETTE
AND HERB CAKES

SLOW-ROASTED TOMATO
AND WATERCRESS SALAD

ORZO PASTA SALAD

GRILLED SARDINES WITH GREMOLATA

TUNA NIÇOISE SALAD

CARROT, CUMIN AND
ORANGE SALAD

MACKEREL CEVICHE WITH SHAVED
FENNEL AND GRAPEFRUIT

QUINOA SALAD

FETA, WATERMELON, CUCUMBER
AND MINT SALAD

GRIDDLED CHICKEN THIGHS
WITH CHICKPEAS, PIQUILLO PEPPERS
AND LEMONY DRESSING

PRAWN AND CUCUMBER SALAD
WITH SPICY YOGHURT DRESSING

SCOTCH EGGS

BEETROOT, CORIANDER SEED
AND ORANGE-CURED SALMON
WITH APPLE AND CELERIAC SALAD

TERIYAKI SALMON

SOBA NOODLE SALAD

ANCHOVY DIP
WITH CRUDITÉS

SERVES 4–6

This punchy dip is a great way of adding interest to a selection of raw vegetables and makes a super healthy lunch or picnic dish. The secret to the anchovy dip is to use the oil from the anchovies as it is packed with flavour. For a richer consistency, you can always blend in a bit of cream or egg yolk. Store any leftovers refrigerated in a Kilner jar for future use.

½ ciabatta loaf, cut into 8 slices
Olive oil
100g jar of best-quality anchovies (drained weight 60g), oil reserved
2 garlic cloves, peeled and chopped
1 banana shallot, peeled and diced
Small handful of parsley
125g pitted black olives
1–2 tsp red wine vinegar
200g radishes, trimmed (or leaves well washed if you keep them on)
Bunch of baby carrots (about 8), tops still on
Sea salt and freshly ground black pepper

1. Preheat the grill.

2. Place the ciabatta on a baking tray, drizzle lightly with olive oil on each side and toast for 6 minutes, turning over halfway through that time, until golden brown and crisp.

3. Meanwhile, put the anchovies, garlic, shallot, parsley and olives into a food processor and whiz until puréed. Add 1 teaspoon of vinegar and a couple of twists of pepper. With the motor running, pour in the reserved anchovy oil (this should be about 4 tablespoons). Now pour in up to 4 tablespoons of olive oil to create your preferred consistency.

4. Taste and adjust the seasoning (and vinegar level) as necessary. If the anchovy dip is too thick, add a little more oil with the motor running. Transfer to a serving dish and place it in the middle of a platter.

5. Arrange the radishes, carrots and toasted ciabatta around the anchovy dip, ready for dipping.

BURRATA WITH QUICK BALSAMIC FIG JAM AND CROSTINI

SERVES 4

Burrata is an extra creamy mozzarella from Puglia in the heel of Italy. It's a beautiful cheese that deserves to be the star attraction, but it has to be eaten when it's very fresh. All you need to go with it are crusty bread, some slow roast tomatoes and torn basil leaves, or perhaps this simple balsamic fig jam.

1 small ciabatta loaf, sliced
3 balls of burrata cheese
Zest of 1 lemon
Olive oil, for drizzling
Sea salt and freshly ground black pepper

FOR THE FIG JAM
150g caster sugar
500g ripe figs, stalks removed, roughly chopped
5 whole star anise
1–2 tbsp balsamic vinegar, to taste

1. First make the fig jam. Sprinkle the sugar, a pinch of salt and the star anise into a heavy-based sauté pan and cook over a medium heat until the sugar begins to caramelise. Add the figs and toss in the caramel. Reduce the heat slightly and add 1 tablespoon of the vinegar. Simmer gently, stirring until the jam has thickened and the figs have almost completely broken down. Remove the star anise.

2. Mash the figs with a potato masher until they have completely collapsed. Take off the heat and set aside to cool.

3. Meanwhile, make the crostini. Preheat a griddle until hot. Drizzle the slices of ciabatta with a little olive oil and season with salt and pepper. Place on the griddle and cook on either side for 1–2 minutes, or until toasted and lightly charred.

4. To serve, place the burrata in a serving bowl, season with salt and pepper, drizzle with olive oil and sprinkle with the lemon zest. Spread the crostini with the fig jam and offer the burrata alongside.

BIG CAESAR SALAD

SERVES 4

Caesar salad is a perennial favourite in our house but with so many mouths to feed, I always have to supersize it. Adding a quickly griddled chicken breast is a simple way of making it stretch further. Coat the croutons in a little dressing before adding them to the lettuce and you'll have explosions of flavour throughout.

150–200g day-old white rustic-style bread
  or sourdough
Olive oil
50g Parmesan cheese
2 romaine lettuce or 4 baby gem lettuce, washed,
  dried, halved and sliced
2 skinless, boneless chicken breasts, butterflied
  (see tip below)
Sea salt and freshly ground black pepper

FOR THE DRESSING
2 free-range egg yolks
1 tsp Dijon mustard
1 tbsp red wine or sherry vinegar
Olive oil
1 x 50g tin best-quality anchovies in olive oil
2 garlic cloves, peeled and finely crushed
75g Parmesan cheese, grated
Juice of 1 lemon, or to taste

HOW TO BUTTERFLY A CHICKEN BREAST
The purpose of butterflying meat is to open it out to make it thinner and quicker to cook. Place the breast on a board and, using a very sharp knife, slice almost all the way through it horizontally – it should remain joined down one side. Then open it like a book, cover with cling film and flatten with a rolling pin until uniformly thin.

1. Chop the bread into 2cm chunks. Lightly drizzle with olive oil and season with a pinch of salt and pepper, then toss to combine.

2. Place a large frying pan over a medium heat, add a dash of oil and fry the bread until golden and crisp. Grate three-quarters of the Parmesan over the croutons, toss together over the heat, then transfer to a plate.

3. To make the dressing, put the egg yolks, mustard and vinegar into a bowl and whisk together. Slowly pour in the olive oil, whisking as you do so, until the mixture emulsifies. Finely chop the anchovies and mix with the garlic to form a rough paste. Add to the dressing and mix well. Stir in the Parmesan, lemon juice to taste, and a little splash of water.

4. Put the lettuce into a serving bowl, add a squeeze of lemon juice and half the dressing. Sprinkle over half the croutons and mix. Top with the rest of the croutons and finish with the remaining Parmesan.

5. Place a griddle pan over a medium–high heat. Season the chicken breasts on both sides, drizzle with a little oil and cook on the hot griddle for 3–4 minutes on either side, until nicely striped and cooked through. Transfer to a plate, sprinkle over some of the remaining dressing and leave to rest for 5 minutes.

6. Slice the chicken into diagonal strips and serve warm, either mixed through or alongside the salad with a little extra dressing spooned over.

HALLOUMI, COURGETTE AND HERB CAKES

SERVES 4

We know halloumi as 'squeaky cheese' in our house because of the noise it makes when you bite into it. The great thing about it is that it holds together well when you cook it, making it ideal for these vegetarian patties. Serve it with the Slow-Roasted Tomato and Watercress Salad (page 112).

2 carrots, peeled and grated
1 courgette, grated
500g halloumi cheese, grated
2–4 spring onions, trimmed and finely chopped
2 tbsp chopped coriander leaves
2 tbsp chopped mint leaves
2 free-range eggs, lightly beaten
2–4 tbsp breadcrumbs
Olive oil, for frying
Sea salt and freshly ground black pepper

FOR THE CHILLI DRESSING
1 red chilli, finely sliced on the diagonal
2 cm piece of fresh root ginger, peeled and finely diced
2 tsp caster sugar
2–3 tbsp rice wine vinegar
2–3 tbsp olive oil
Pinch of salt

HOW TO CHOP HERBS
Soft herbs, such as basil, parsley, coriander and mint, can bruise very easily, so try to ensure you cut them only once. The easiest way to do this is to roll them gently into a ball or cigar shape, and slice along their length. Don't be tempted to go back over them – unlike rosemary, say, they never have to be cut that fine.

1. To make the halloumi cakes put the carrots and courgette in a sieve or colander and sprinkle with a decent pinch of salt to draw out the moisture. Place over a bowl to drain for 5 minutes, then tip into a clean tea towel and squeeze out all the excess water.

2. Put the halloumi, carrot mixture, spring onions, coriander and mint into a bowl, season and mix together. Add the beaten eggs and mix well, then stir in 2 tablespoons of the breadcrumbs. The mixture should be sticky enough to form into patties, if it's not sticky enough add some more breadcrumbs. Shape the mixture into 8 larger patties about 1cm thick, or 16 smaller ones. To help shape the patties place a large spoonful of the mix onto a spoon and press against your hand and squeeze out any excess liquid. Leave in the fridge uncovered for at least 20–25 minutes to firm up.

3. Meanwhile, put all the dressing ingredients into a bowl and stir well until the sugar has dissolved. Taste and adjust the seasoning as necessary.

4. Once you're ready to cook, heat a large heavy-based frying pan over a medium heat. Add a dash of oil and fry the halloumi cakes (in batches if necessary) until dark golden and crisp on either side and hot all the way through.

5. Serve the cakes hot with spoonfuls of the chilli dressing over the top.

SLOW-ROASTED TOMATO AND WATERCRESS SALAD

SERVES 4

Tomatoes, watercress and shallots – one of the simplest combinations, but the flavours work so well together. Especially if you've taken the trouble to slow roast the tomatoes first to intensify their flavour. I sometimes do these in large batches and keep them in olive oil in the fridge for adding to sandwiches or other salads. The perfect accompaniment to my Halloumi, Courgette, and Herb Cakes (page 110). Photograph previous page.

300g cherry tomatoes, in a mixture of colours
  if you wish, cut in half
2 thyme sprigs, leaves only
2 garlic cloves, peeled and finely sliced
Caster sugar, for sprinkling
Olive oil, for drizzling
125g watercress, well washed
½ banana shallot, sliced into rings
Aged balsamic vinegar, for drizzling
Sea salt and freshly ground black pepper

1. Preheat the oven to 150°C/Gas 2.

2. Arrange the tomatoes in a single layer, cut side up, in a baking tray. Sprinkle over the thyme leaves, garlic and a couple of pinches of sugar. Season with salt and pepper and drizzle with oil.

3. Place in the oven for 1–1½ hours, until the tomatoes have shrivelled up.

4. Once ready to serve, place the watercress in a serving bowl, add the shallot rings and tomatoes and mix well. Drizzle with a little olive oil and a couple of splashes of balsamic vinegar to taste. Season and serve.

HOW TO VARY THE RECIPE
If you don't have any shallots to hand, you can use thinly sliced onions. Soak them in milk or salted water for 20 minutes first to make them less astringent.

ORZO PASTA SALAD
SERVES 4

The pepperiness of the rocket, the perfume of the basil and the acidity of the dressing work beautifully together in this salad. Orzo looks like barley, but is actually made of pasta. It's traditionally used to add body to soups and casseroles but works equally well here. Adding a bay leaf to the cooking water gives it an intriguing background flavour. This salad works well with Griddled Sardines with Gremolata (page 114). Photograph overleaf.

200g orzo
1 bay leaf
50–100g pine nuts
Large bunch of basil, chopped
100g rocket, roughly chopped
Olive oil, for drizzling
Sea salt and freshly ground black pepper

FOR THE DRESSING
30g Parmesan cheese, finely grated
Zest of 1 lemon
6 tbsp extra virgin olive oil

1. Cook the orzo according to the packet instructions, but adding the bay leaf to the cooking water. When al dente, drain, then hold under running cold water for about 10 seconds to stop the cooking process. Discard the bay leaf, then drizzle the orzo with a little olive oil and mix it through to stop the grains sticking together.

2. Meanwhile, make the dressing in your serving bowl. Mix the Parmesan with the lemon zest and juice. Add 3 tablespoons of the oil and mix well. Taste and season as necessary, adding a little more oil if needed.

3. Toast the pine nuts in a dry frying pan over a medium heat until golden. Remove and set aside until cool.

4. While the orzo is still slightly warm, add it to the dressing then mix through the rocket, basil and pine nuts. Taste and adjust the seasoning as necessary, and serve.

HOW TO ZEST CITRUS FRUIT
Place a four-sided grater on a plate. Using the side with the smallest holes, rub the fruit down it in long, sweeping strokes, turning the fruit a little after each stroke so you don't grate any of the bitter white pith.

GRIDDLED SARDINES WITH GREMOLATA
SERVES 4

I love sardines: they are such a healthy but under-rated fish. My favourite way of eating them is charred and blistered from a beachside barbecue, but failing that, this recipe is pretty special too. Gremolata is a typical Italian condiment made of lemon zest, garlic and parsley which is served with fish or grilled meats. I've added a little orange here too as it works so well with the sardines. The Orzo Pasta Salad on page 113 will go with this perfectly.

12–16 sardines (depending on size), scaled and gutted
Olive oil, for drizzling
Bunch of rosemary – 12–16 sprigs
Sea salt and freshly ground black pepper

FOR THE GREMOLATA
Bunch of parsley, leaves only, chopped
Zest and juice of 1 lemon
Zest and juice of ½ orange
1 garlic clove, peeled and finely grated or crushed
Olive oil

1. Drizzle the sardines with a little olive oil and season with salt. Insert a small sprig of rosemary in the stomach cavity of each one.

2. Place a griddle pan over a high heat. When hot, add the sardines (in batches if necessary) and cook for 2–3 minutes on each side, until nicely marked and cooked through.

3. Meanwhile, put the parsley in a bowl, add the citrus zest and juice, the garlic and a drizzle of olive oil. Stir well, then taste and season with a pinch of salt and pepper if necessary.

4. Serve the sardines with the gremolata spooned on top.

TUNA NIÇOISE SALAD

SERVES 4

This is a classic French salad, which you'll often see smartened up in restaurants with freshly seared tuna, but I think it is much better made the way the French intended, with tinned. With its ripe tomatoes and naturally black olives, it's full of the flavours of Provence. The only twist I like to do is to incorporate the anchovies into the dressing rather than laying them on top. That way you get to enjoy the lovely salty kick throughout the salad. A perfect accompaniment to this salad is the Pear, Goat's Cheese and Walnut Tartine (page 82).

8 new potatoes (halved or quartered if large)
500g green beans, trimmed
Extra virgin olive oil, for drizzling
4 free-range eggs
2 baby gem lettuce, cut into wedges
320g best-quality tinned tuna in olive oil, drained and flaked
75g black olives, preferably French, roughly torn
250g baby plum tomatoes, halved
Sea salt and freshly ground black pepper

FOR THE DRESSING
1 tsp Dijon mustard
1 tbsp capers
5 best-quality anchovies in olive oil
1 garlic clove, peeled and roughly chopped
2 tbsp red wine vinegar
4 tablespoons extra virgin olive oil
Small handful of parsley leaves, finely chopped

1. Put the potatoes into a pan of cold water with a pinch of salt, bring to the boil, then boil for 6–7 minutes. Add the green beans and continue to boil for 3–5 minutes, or until both the potatoes and beans are tender. Drain in a colander, then season and drizzle with a little oil. Set aside.

2. Meanwhile, boil the eggs in gently boiling water for 7 minutes, or until almost hard-boiled. Drain, then fill the pan with cold water, tap the eggs against the side to crack the shells and leave to sit in the water to cool.

3. To make the dressing, put the mustard, capers, anchovies and 2 teaspoons of their oil into a mortar and pound to a paste. Add the garlic and a good pinch of pepper and mix again. Finally, add the vinegar, olive oil and parsley and mix well.

4. Halve the potatoes, then peel and slice the eggs.

5. To serve, place 2 tablespoons of the dressing on a large serving platter or in a shallow bowl. Arrange the ingredients as you prefer, drizzling with the dressing as you go. Finish with the remaining dressing.

HOW TO CHOOSE BLACK OLIVES
Always try to buy genuinely black olives, which have been left on the trees to ripen naturally and are actually more of a dark greeny brown. The uniformly glossy black ones you often see are simply green olives painted with a black dye.

CARROT, CUMIN AND ORANGE SALAD

SERVES 4

This is a lovely sunny-looking salad typical of Morocco. It's also that rare thing – a salad that gets better for standing around a bit and allowing the flavours to mingle. Serve with grilled meat or fish.

5 carrots, peeled and grated
Zest and juice of 1 orange
75g pumpkin seeds
50g sunflower seeds
1½ tsp cumin seeds, toasted
1 tbsp Dijon mustard
1 tbsp runny honey
1 tbsp white wine vinegar
3–4 tbsp olive oil
2 tbsp torn coriander leaves
2 tbsp torn mint leaves
Sea salt

1. Mix the carrots in a bowl with the orange zest and juice, the pumpkin and sunflower seeds.

2. Grind the cumin seeds with a little sea salt using a pestle and mortar, then stir them into the carrot mixture.

3. Combine the mustard, honey, vinegar and olive oil in a bowl. Add the mint and coriander leaves, then taste and adjust the seasoning as necessary. Pour over the salad and toss well. This can be eaten straight away, or will keep for up to 2 days in the fridge.

MACKEREL CEVICHE WITH SHAVED FENNEL AND GRAPEFRUIT

SERVES 4

Ceviche is a South American dish of raw fish marinated in a mixture of citrus juice and herbs and spices. It is incredibly light and healthy, especially when made with an oily fish like mackerel, which is full of omega 3. Make sure you use the freshest fish you can find and don't dress it until you are ready to eat or it will 'cook' in the grapefruit juice and go mushy. This is lovely served alongside Quinoa Salad (page 122).

2 pink grapefruit
Olive oil, for drizzling
1 fennel bulb, with fronds if available
2 mackerel fillets, extremely fresh, pin-boned
Small bunch of coriander, leaves chopped
Zest and juice of 1 lime
Sea salt and freshly ground black pepper

1. First make the salad. Finely grate the grapefruit zest and set it aside. Cut off and discard the skin and pith. Segment the flesh by slicing it between the membrane and place it in a bowl. Squeeze over the juices from any bits of flesh still attached to the membrane, season with salt and pepper, add a drizzle of olive oil and mix together.

2. Arrange the grapefruit in concentric circles on a serving plate, reserving the dressing in the bowl.

3. Roughly chop the fennel fronds and set aside. Peel off and discard the outer layer of the fennel, then use a peeler or mandoline to cut thin strips from the bulb. Place in a bowl of iced water for 5–10 minutes to crisp up.

4. Meanwhile, make the ceviche. Spoon half the grapefruit dressing over a serving plate. Cut the mackerel into slices 5mm thick and place them on top of the dressing. Season with a pinch of salt and pepper, then sprinkle with half the grapefruit zest, coriander and fennel fronds.

5. Drain the fennel and dry with kitchen paper. Place it on top of the grapefruit and sprinkle with the remaining grapefruit zest, coriander, fennel fronds, lime zest and juice. Season with a pinch of salt and the remaining grapefruit dressing. Drizzle with a little more olive oil and serve with the ceviche.

QUINOA SALAD
SERVES 4

Quinoa is a slightly nutty grain that makes a great alternative to couscous, rice or lentils. Here I've turned it into a simple salad, based on a very popular dish we serve at Bread Street Kitchen. If you are serving this with the Mackerel Ceviche with Shaved Fennel and Grapefruit (page 120), you could dress it with the same marinade. Photograph on previous page.

200g quinoa
50g flaked almonds
½ large cucumber
125g cherry tomatoes, halved
50g raisins
4 spring onions, trimmed and finely chopped
Bunch of mint, leaves only
Juice of 1 lime
Olive oil, for drizzling
Sea salt and freshly ground black pepper

1. Cook the quinoa according to the packet instructions, then drain and spread out on a large plate or tray to cool quickly.

2. Toast the almonds in a dry frying pan until golden and place in a salad bowl.

3. Using a vegetable peeler, take lengthways strips of skin off the cucumber so that it looks stripy. Cut it in half lengthways, then spoon out and discard the seeds. Chop the cucumber into half-moon slices and add to the almonds in the salad bowl.

4. Add the tomatoes, raisins, spring onions and half the mint to the bowl. Then add the cooked quinoa and mix everything together. Season well with salt and pepper. Dress the salad with the lime juice and a good drizzle of olive oil.

5. Taste and adjust the seasoning as necessary. Garnish with the remaining mint leaves and serve.

FETA, WATERMELON, CUCUMBER AND MINT SALAD
SERVES 4

Unusual as this salad sounds, it really works because of the pairing of salty feta with sweet watermelon. In Greece, where it originates, they'll often throw in some black olives too but I like the crunch you get from the toasted pecans. Don't make this salad ahead or the salty cheese and nuts will draw the moisture out of the watermelon, making them all soggy. Pair this salad with Griddled Chicken Thighs with Chick Peas, Piquillo Peppers and Lemony Dressing (page 122) Photograph overleaf.

50g whole pecan nuts
1 ripe watermelon, flesh cut into chunks, any seeds and white parts discarded
1 cucumber, peeled, deseeded and chopped into chunks
200g best-quality feta cheese
Extra virgin olive oil, for drizzling
Small bunch of mint, leaves only, roughly chopped
1 tsp ground sumac
Juice of 1 lemon
Sea salt and freshly ground black pepper

1. Break up the pecans and lightly toast in a dry frying pan with a pinch of salt until golden. Remove and lightly crush in a pestle and mortar. Leave to cool.

2. Place the watermelon in a serving bowl and mix in the cucumber. Crumble in the feta and mix well, seasoning with a little salt and pepper and a drizzle of olive oil. Add the mint leaves, pecans, sumac and lemon juice to taste. Toss lightly and serve.

GRIDDLED CHICKEN THIGHS WITH CHICKPEAS, PIQUILLO PEPPERS AND LEMONY DRESSING

SERVES 4

Don't automatically turn to chicken breasts over other parts of the bird. Chicken thighs are fantastically tasty too, and because they are richer and more robust, they can stand up to punchy flavours better. With its mix of chickpeas, capers and piquillo peppers, this is casual Spanish cooking at its best and would be a great summery meal served with the Feta, Watermelon, Cucumber and Mint Salad on page 123. Photograph overleaf.

4 boneless chicken thighs, skin on
Olive oil, for drizzling
1 x 200g jar piquillo or roasted red peppers, drained, cut into strips
1 x 400g tin cooked chickpeas, drained
8–12 caper berries, stalks removed, halved
Small bunch of basil, leaves only, roughly torn
Sea salt and freshly ground black pepper

FOR THE DRESSING
1 tsp Dijon mustard
4 tbsp extra virgin olive oil
Juice of 1 lemon

1. Place a griddle pan over a high heat. Put the chicken on a plate and drizzle with a little olive oil. Season with salt and pepper and toss well to coat. Place in the hot griddle pan, skin side down, and cook for 4–5 minutes, until the skin is dark golden, crisp and marked with griddle lines. Lower the heat and turn the chicken over. Cook for a further 6–8 minutes, turning now and again, until the chicken is cooked through. Remove and set aside to rest for a few minutes.

2. To make the dressing put the mustard into a bowl, add the olive oil, lemon juice and salt and pepper. Mix well, then taste and adjust the seasoning as necessary.

3. Place the peppers strips, chickpeas and caper berries in a salad bowl and mix well. Taste and adjust the seasoning as necessary.

4. Mix the basil into the chickpea salad, then pour in three-quarters of the dressing. Slice the chicken into chunky slices and place on top of the salad. Toss lightly, drizzle over the remaining dressing and serve.

HOW TO GRIDDLE
Whenever you use a griddle pan, always press down hard what you are cooking and hold it there for a few seconds. This will help achieve those characteristic scorch lines, which not only look attractive but mean more flavour.

GRIDDLED CHICKEN THIGHS WITH CHICKPEAS, PIQUILLO PEPPERS
AND LEMONY DRESSING (RECIPE PAGE 123)

FETA, WATERMELON, CUCUMBER
AND MINT SALAD (RECIPE PAGE 122)

PRAWN AND CUCUMBER SALAD
WITH SPICY YOGHURT DRESSING

SERVES 4

I used to love prawn cocktails in the Seventies, but to modern tastes that mix of ketchup and mayonnaise is too heavy and gloopy. This Asian-inspired version is made with natural yoghurt, sweet chilli and lime and is much lighter and healthier. It's a great dish for picnics, if you're heading outdoors with it make the dressing in a jar with a tight fitting lid. As with all leaf-based salads, you should only dress it at the last minute to avoid the leaves wilting.

400g king prawns, cooked and peeled
1 large cucumber, peeled, deseeded and sliced
2 baby gem lettuces, shredded

FOR THE DRESSING
1–1½ tbsp fish sauce, to taste
2 tbsp sweet chilli sauce
Zest and juice of 1 lime
1 tsp golden caster sugar
4 tbsp natural yoghurt

1. First make the dressing. Place 1 tablespoon of the fish sauce in a bowl (or a jar if you are taking this on a picnic) and add the chilli sauce, lime zest and juice and the sugar. Mix well. Add the yoghurt a spoonful at a time, stirring as you do so, then taste and add a little more fish sauce if needed.

2. Place 1 tablespoon of the dressing in a salad bowl. Sit the prawns, cucumber and lettuce on top. Cover and set aside (in the fridge if not required for a few hours).

3. Just before serving, pour the remaining dressing over the salad and toss well.

SCOTCH EGGS

SERVES 4

Scotch eggs are the ultimate all-in-one snack, delicious on their own or served with a spoonful of chutney. The black pudding and grated apple work really well together and take this simple picnic food to another level. Make sure you use flaky panko breadcrumbs as this is the secret of a lovely crispy golden coating.

6 free-range eggs
200g best-quality sausage meat
200g best-quality black pudding, skin removed,
   meat crumbled
½ Granny Smith apple, grated
4 tbsp plain flour
150g panko breadcrumbs
Flavourless oil, e.g. groundnut or sunflower,
   for deep-frying
Sea salt and freshly ground black pepper

1. Place 4 of the eggs in a pan of boiling water and boil for 4½ minutes. Drain, then fill the pan with cold water, tap the eggs against the side to crack the shells and leave to sit in the water to cool.

2. Meanwhile, mix together the sausage meat, black pudding and apple until well combined. Divide the mixture into 4 equal pieces and shape into flattened ovals.

3. Place the flour in a shallow dish and season with salt and pepper. Beat the remaining 2 eggs in another dish, and place the breadcrumbs in a third shallow dish.

4. Peel the boiled eggs, then place each one in the middle of a sausage meat oval and press the mixture around them until they are evenly covered.

5. Pour a 4cm depth of oil into a sauté pan and heat until it begins to shimmer.

6. Meanwhile, dust the meat-covered eggs in flour, shaking off any excess. Roll in the beaten egg, allowing any excess to drip off. Finally, coat in the breadcrumbs, pressing them in so that they really stick.

7. Shallow-fry the eggs for 10–12 minutes, turning often, until golden and crisp on the outside and cooked through inside. Serve warm or cold.

HOW TO PEEL A HARD-BOILED EGG
The easiest way is to crack the shell and then leave it in cold water for a couple of minutes. The water will seep inside the shell, making it easy to slip off.

BEETROOT, CORIANDER SEED AND ORANGE-CURED SALMON WITH APPLE AND CELERIAC SALAD

SERVES 8–10

Salmon was a luxury when I was growing up but nowadays it has become almost commonplace, so here's a recipe to put the excitement back into it. The outside of the salmon takes on the deep red of the beetroot and looks stunning once it is sliced. The apple and celeriac salad is based on the classic French salad, remoulade, but I've added the matchsticks of apple to counter the sharpness of the lemon. Put the salmon and salad together and it's a match made in heaven.

800g middle piece of salmon side,
   scaled but skin on
Rye bread, toasted, to serve

FOR THE CURE
2 tbsp coriander seeds
250g raw beetroot, peeled and grated
Zest of 2 oranges
100g fine sea salt
100g caster sugar
Freshly ground black pepper

FOR THE APPLE AND CELERIAC SALAD
Juice of 1 lemon
1 large, firm celeriac, peeled
2–3 Granny Smith apples (depending on size),
   quartered and cored
300ml sour cream
2 tbsp good-quality mayonnaise
Small bunch of parsley, leaves only, finely chopped
Sea salt and freshly ground black pepper
2 tbsp poppy seeds, to garnish

1. Take a baking dish or roasting tray large enough to fit the salmon and line it with cling film. Trim the sides of the salmon if necessary to neaten the edges, then place in the dish, skin side down.

2. To make the cure, break up the coriander seeds using a mortar and pestle. Place in a bowl with the beetroot, orange zest, fine sea salt, sugar and a couple of twists of black pepper and mix well.

3. Spread the cure mixture over the salmon, making sure the flesh is completely covered. Cover with a sheet of cling film and sit another dish or tray directly on top of that. Weigh this down with some tins or a heavy pan and leave in the fridge for 8 hours or overnight.

4. Meanwhile, make the salad. Put the lemon juice into a large bowl. Slice the celeriac and apple into matchsticks, and toss immediately in the lemon juice to prevent them from going brown.

5. In a separate bowl, mix together the sour cream, mayonnaise and parsley. Season with salt and pepper, then add to the celeriac and mix well. Taste and adjust the seasoning as necessary.

6. Once ready to serve, remove the salmon from the cure, wiping off any excess. Place the fish on a chopping board, skin side down, and thinly slice the flesh at an angle into pieces about 1–2mm thick, flicking your knife when you reach the skin to slice the flesh away from it. Transfer the salmon pieces to a plate.

7. Garnish the apple and celeriac salad with the poppy seeds and serve alongside the sliced salmon with some toasted rye bread.

TERIYAKI SALMON

SERVES 4

Given how much salmon we eat at home, I'm always trying out new ways of serving it, and this is my current favourite. It's amazing how much flavour the salmon takes on after just 20 minutes in the sweet and salty marinade, and it's even better if you can give it two hours. Remember always to cook fish skin-side down at first to protect the delicate flesh from too much heat. Serve with garlic tenderstem broccoli and perhaps Soba Noodle Salad (see page 133). Photograph overleaf.

2cm piece of fresh root ginger, finely sliced
2 garlic cloves, peeled and finely sliced
3 tbsp soy sauce
2 tbsp maple syrup
1 tbsp mirin (rice wine)
Olive oil
4 salmon fillets (about 500g in total)
Sea salt and freshly ground pepper

1. Put the ginger and garlic into a bowl and mix with the soy sauce, maple syrup, mirin and a drizzle of olive oil.

2. Place the salmon fillets in a dish, season with salt and pepper and pour the sticky dressing over them. Cover with cling film and set aside in the fridge to marinate for up to 2 hours, but at least 20 minutes.

3. Place a large frying pan over a medium heat and add a dash of oil. When hot, add the salmon, skin side down, reserving the marinade. Cook for 2 minutes, then pour in the reserved marinade and cook for a further minute or so, until the salmon fillets are opaque halfway up the sides. Turn them over and cook on the other side for 3–4 minutes, basting with the sauce so that the salmon is well coated. Add a splash of water if the sauce is too thick.

4. Serve the salmon fillets on individual plates, spooning over any teriyaki sauce left in the pan.

SOBA NOODLE SALAD
SERVES 4

A wholesome, filling side dish of buckwheat noodles served with fresh vegetables and dressed with a kind of Japanese vinaigrette of sesame oil, rice vinegar, soy sauce and lemon juice. Do add the nori seaweed if you can. It gives the finished dish a real depth of flavour. A perfect dish to accompany Teriyaki Salmon (page 132). Photograph overleaf.

300g soba noodles
100g kale, stalks removed, leaves shredded or torn
150g sugarsnap peas, topped and tailed,
   halved lengthways
3 carrots, peeled and sliced into ribbons
   (use a vegetable peeler)
2 spring onions, trimmed and finely chopped
3cm piece of fresh root ginger, peeled and
   finely sliced
1 tbsp sesame oil
1–2 tsp rice vinegar
1–1½ tbsp soy sauce
Juice of ½ lemon
1 sheet of nori seaweed, finely sliced (optional)
Sea salt and freshly ground pepper

1. Cook the soba noodles according to the packet instructions. When almost cooked, add the kale, sugarsnaps and carrots to the pan to blanch. Drain once the noodles are tender.

2. Add all the remaining ingredients to the noodle mixture, season with a little salt and pepper, stir well and serve.

TERIYAKI SALMON (RECIPE PAGE 132)

SOBA NOODLE SALAD (RECIPE PAGE 133)

AFTERNOON PICK-ME-UPS

EVERYONE NEEDS A LITTLE SWEET SOMETHING EVERY NOW AND AGAIN.

Whether as a treat in a lunchbox or as part of an old-fashioned tea-time spread. My mum ran a tea-room in Stratford upon Avon when I was growing up, and the smell of cakes and biscuits as they come out of the oven still takes me right back. For a lot of us, this was where we first tried our hand at cooking, helping to make a Victoria sponge or tray of flapjacks and getting to lick the bowl afterwards. It's certainly a great way to get children interested. It's important for them to learn that cooking savoury food can be just as rewarding, but that a sweet treat won't do you any harm as long as it is an occasional indulgence. All of my children have enjoyed rolling up their sleeves and getting stuck in.

We've got a good repertoire of cakes and biscuits in this country, but in this chapter I wanted to explore some recipes from other countries such as America, France and Turkey. It always amazes me how different nations can put different twists on things. None of these recipes have to be eaten at tea-time, of course. The Lemon and Poppy Seed Madeleines on page 145, for example, are great at breakfast, too, and I can't imagine anyone complaining about being served a slice of Chocolate and Mint Caramel cake for pudding.

Whereas in most savoury cooking you can experiment with the proportions, adding less or more of each ingredient according to taste, with baking you do have to be more precise. Baking is a science, in which the ingredients react against each other to achieve the result you want – the rise of a sponge, for example – and you mess with the proportions at your peril. If you do have trouble with a recipe that hasn't performed the way you expected, this is always the first thing to check. Did you weigh everything out properly? Overleaf are a few more tips that will apply either to these recipes or more general baking.

BAKING TINS

Buy the heaviest you can as they will heat up evenly. To prevent food sticking, either butter and line them with greaseproof paper, or butter and dust them with flour. You can also get silicone muffin trays nowadays, which are very easy to turn out, but you can't use them to make other things like Yorkshire puddings, obviously.

BUTTER

I prefer to use unsalted butter in my sweet cooking as I find it creams better and it also means that if I want to add a pinch of salt (which helps to accentuate the sweetness) I am in control of how much to add. One of the most important things when making a cake is to have all your ingredients at room temperature. If your butter is too hard, it won't cream properly and then you will struggle to incorporate the air it needs to rise. Don't put it in the microwave, but you can cut it into cubes and put it in lukewarm water for a few minutes.

FLOUR

Plain flour is made from wheat, but you can experiment with different types. A little chestnut flour works beautifully in cakes. I'm a great fan of wholemeal or spelt flours, which retain more of the husk. They tend to be a bit heavier than plain flour but can give a nice nuttiness to biscuits or muffins. If you want your dish to rise, for example, in a muffin or American pancake, you will need to use self-raising flour, which is plain flour with baking powder added. Plain flour will keep indefinitely, but self-raising does have a use-by date because the rising agents will become less effective with time. If you want to make your own self-raising flour, add 2 teaspoons of baking powder to every 150g of plain flour and mix well.

GOLDEN SYRUP

A great addition to biscuits as it adds a chewiness to the finished texture. You can also add a spoonful to your sugar when making caramel as it interferes with the formation of sugar crystals which can make your caramel seize.

SUGAR

Different sugars all have different qualities. Muscovado is sticky and treacly, so great for biscuits, fruit cakes and pickles. Powdery icing sugar dissolves easily so is ideal for buttercreams and icings. Palm sugar, made from palm tree sap, usually comes as a paste and adds a caramelly flavour to sweet and savoury Asian dishes. Demerara has larger crystals to add crunch to things like cookies, crumbles and flapjacks. And then there is caster sugar, halfway between granulated and icing sugar and the ultimate for baking.

WORKING WITH PASTRY

You should always chill pastry after it has been rolled out into the tart tin to prevent it from shrinking in the oven. If you are going to be adding a runny filling that will make the pastry soggy, recipes usually call for it be blind baked. This means filling the case with ceramic baking beans (or lentils or rice) to weigh the pastry base down and stop it puffing up. Normally after about 15 minutes' cooking, you will remove the beans and continue to blind bake the case until it is golden. Now you can add the filling and return it to the oven without fear of the pastry being soggy on the bottom.

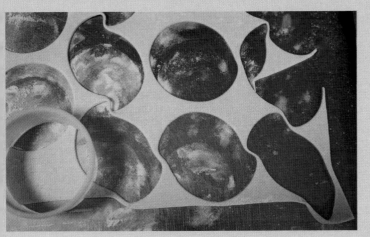

LEMON AND POPPY SEED MADELEINES

PEAR AND CRUNCHY GRANOLA MUFFINS

PEANUT BUTTER AND JAM COOKIES

DULCE DE LECHE BISCUITS

CRANBERRY, MARSHMALLOW AND
PEANUT CHOCOLATE FRIDGE CAKE

LEMON AND PISTACHIO BAKLAVA

CHOCOLATE AND MINT CARAMEL CAKE

SALTED CARAMEL POPCORN

LEMON AND POPPY
SEED MADELEINES
MAKES 16

I fell in love with these delicate sponge cakes when I worked in France and would often treat myself to a couple for breakfast after a night shift making bread. The batter will keep in the fridge overnight if you want to bake them first thing in the morning (don't forget to mix the batter again first); otherwise, they make a great tea-time treat. If you don't have a madeleine pan, you can always use a small muffin tin, but bear in mind that the sponges won't have that lovely shell shape that makes them so special.

75g unsalted butter, melted and cooled slightly, plus softened butter for greasing
2 tbsp plain flour, for dusting
75g caster sugar
3 free-range eggs
75g self-raising flour
1½ tbsp poppy seeds
Finely grated zest of 2 lemons

1. Preheat the oven to 180°C/Gas 4. Brush 2 madeleine trays with softened butter, dust with sifted plain flour, then tap out the excess.

2. Place the sugar and eggs in a large bowl and whisk together for at least 5 minutes, or until pale, thick and the mixture holds a trail on the surface when the beaters are lifted.

3. Carefully sift the self-raising flour over the egg mixture, then sprinkle with the poppy seeds and lemon zest. Pour the melted butter down the inside edge of the bowl and, using a spatula, quickly and gently fold the ingredients together. Be careful not to knock out too much air.

4. Transfer the batter to a jug and pour some into each indent of the prepared trays, filling them to the top. Bake for 8–10 minutes.

5. Transfer the madeleines to a wire rack and leave to cool. They are at their best when served warm.

HOW TO MAKE THE PERFECT SPONGE
The secret of a light, airy sponge is to incorporate lots of air into your mix. It is essential that you whisk together the eggs and sugar together for a good five minutes on full speed, until it is thick and pale. Time invested now will immeasurably improve the end result.

PEAR AND CRUNCHY GRANOLA MUFFINS

MAKES 16

The American muffin has well and truly taken over from its doughy English counterpart, and since spending more time in the States, the whole family has developed a taste for them. I like these ones because they aren't as sweet as some and the crunchy muesli topping gives them an even healthier feel. And the beauty of this recipe is that you can make the batter, refrigerate it the night before you need it, then mix it again in the morning and bake! Great at any time of day, from breakfast through elevenses to afternoon tea.

300g self-raising flour, sifted
1 tsp baking powder
1 tsp ground cinnamon
Pinch of sea salt
125g light muscovado sugar
250ml whole milk
2 free-range eggs, beaten
100g butter, melted
2 small ripe pears, peeled, cored and cut into
    small pieces
100g crunchy granola

1. Preheat the oven to 180°C/Gas 4 and line a couple of muffin trays with paper cases.

2. Sift the flour, baking powder, cinnamon and salt into a large bowl, then stir in the sugar. Whisk the milk, eggs and butter together in a large jug, then pour into the dry ingredients and mix well. Stir in the pears and half the granola.

3. Divide the batter between the muffin cases, and sprinkle the top of each one with the remaining granola.

4. Bake for 25–30 minutes, or until a skewer inserted into the middle of the muffins comes out clean. Leave to cool for 5 minutes before serving warm or at room temperature.

HOW TO MAKE PERFECT MUFFINS
Don't overmix your wet and dry ingredients. A couple of stirs with a spoon will be plenty – or, better still, use your hands. Otherwise the muffins will come out heavy.

PEANUT BUTTER AND JAM COOKIES
MAKES 30

Another American-inspired combo. I used to love peanut butter and jam sandwiches for tea when I was young – much to my mum's horror – and the flavours work just as well in a chewy cookie. This is a great one for getting the kids involved. They love rolling out the balls of dough and then making indents with their tiny fingers so you can add a dollop of jam and peanut butter.

185g plain flour, sifted
1 tsp baking powder
Pinch of sea salt
125g butter, softened
325g peanut butter (smooth or crunchy is fine)
185g light muscovado sugar
3 tbsp milk
1 vanilla pod, split open and seeds scraped out
1 large free-range egg, beaten
125g raspberry jam

1. Preheat the oven to 180°C/Gas 4 and line 2 baking sheets with baking paper.

2. Sift the flour, baking powder and salt into a bowl.

3. Put the butter, 200g of the peanut butter and the sugar into a large separate bowl and whisk until pale and fluffy. Add the milk, vanilla seeds and egg and beat until smooth. Gradually sift in the flour mixture and beat until combined.

4. Using lightly floured hands, roll the dough into 30 balls slightly smaller than a walnut, gently flatten them and place them on the prepared baking sheets. Using 1 or 2 fingers, press down in the middle of each one to make a shallow indent. Place a ½ teaspoon of jam and a ½ teaspoon of peanut butter in each indent.

5. Bake for 10–12 minutes, until pale golden. Using a spatula, transfer the biscuits to a wire rack to cool before serving.

DULCE DE LECHE BISCUITS

MAKES 8

Also known as 'alfajores', these crumbly shortbread biscuits are popular all over South America, from Argentina to Peru. They were brought over by the Spanish, who in turn were introduced to them by the Moors of North Africa. The secret of their more-ishness (sorry!) is the dulce de leche (sweet caramel) used to sandwich the biscuits together. If you want to take them to another level, roll them in desiccated coconut around the edges just before serving.

150g granulated sugar
250g salted butter, softened
1 large free-range egg
1 vanilla pod, split open and seeds scraped out
250g plain flour, plus extra for rolling
90g cornflour
½ tsp baking powder
250g dulce de leche or condensed milk caramel
Icing sugar, for dusting

1. Preheat the oven to 180°C/Gas 4. Line 2 baking sheets with baking paper.

2. Put the sugar and butter into a bowl and beat with an electric whisk until light and fluffy. Beat in the egg and vanilla seeds.

3. Sift the flour, cornflour and baking powder over the butter mixture and mix together until a dough forms.

4. Using lightly floured hands, divide the dough into 16 equal pieces and roll into balls. Place them on the prepared sheets, spacing them well apart, then press down with the palm of your hand to flatten slightly. Chill for 10 minutes or until firm to touch.

5. Bake for 10–12 minutes, until the biscuits are pale golden. Using a spatula, transfer them to a wire rack to cool.

6. When cold, sandwich the flat sides of the biscuits together with a tablespoon of dulce de leche, and dust with icing sugar to serve.

HOW TO MAKE DULCE DE LECHE
Dulce de leche is available in most supermarkets. To make your own, pierce the top of a can of condensed milk in two places and then place it in simmering water, being careful the water doesn't come to the top of the can, for three to four hours. Leave to cool before opening.

CRANBERRY, MARSHMALLOW AND PEANUT CHOCOLATE FRIDGE CAKE

MAKES 14 PIECES

A fridge cake, or tiffin, as it is also known, is perfect for making with children because it doesn't need baking. Feel free to experiment with any combination of dried fruit and nuts you like: raisins, cherries, blueberries, walnuts and hazelnuts would all work well. You can also store this in the freezer, making it the perfect cake to take on a picnic. Simply put it in a chiller bag where it will act as an ice pack until you are ready to slice it.

100g butter, cubed
300g milk or dark chocolate, as you prefer
4 tbsp golden syrup
200g digestive biscuits
75g mini marshmallows
75g dried cranberries
75g salted peanuts, roughly chopped

1. Lightly grease and line a 16 x 26mm baking tray with greaseproof or baking paper, leaving a generous overhang so that the paper will cover the top of the finished cake.

2. Gently melt the butter, chocolate and golden syrup in a saucepan over a low heat. Remove from the heat immediately and allow to cool slightly.

3. Meanwhile, place the digestives in a mixing bowl and break into small chunks.

4. Stir the biscuits, marshmallows, cranberries and peanuts together. Pour in the chocolate mixture and mix well. Spoon into the prepared baking tray and press down with a spatula. Fold the overhanging paper over the top of the cake and using your hands press down hard to compact the mixture, then place in the fridge to set. Alternatively, place in the freezer and store until wanted.

5. To serve, remove from the baking tray and slice into pieces.

LEMON AND PISTACHIO BAKLAVA

MAKES 16–20 PIECES

The classic Middle Eastern tea-time treat of layers of chopped nuts interlaced with flaky filo pastry and finished off in sugar syrup. The lemon helps to cut through the sweetness but I'm not going to pretend that this is anything other than very indulgent. Best served with tea or coffee.

300g unsalted pistachio nuts, chopped
   (you may find this easiest to do in a blender)
100g caster sugar
Zest of 1 lemon
200g butter, melted
16 sheets of filo pastry, cut in half

FOR THE SYRUP
200g caster sugar
Zest and juice of 1 lemon

1. Preheat the oven to 160°C/Gas 3.

2. Put the pistachios, caster sugar and lemon zest into a bowl and mix together.

3. Select a baking tray the size of your halved filo sheets. Brush it with melted butter and place a halved sheet of filo on it. Brush this with butter, sprinkle with some of the pistachio mixture, and continue layering the sheets in the same way until you have used all 32 of them.

4. Using a sharp knife, cut the layered pastry into bite-sized squares. Bake for 30–40 minutes, until golden and crisp on top.

5. Meanwhile, make the syrup. Put the sugar, lemon zest and juice into a small saucepan with 200ml water and bring to the boil, stirring to help the sugar dissolve. Simmer for 7–10 minutes, until the syrup has slightly thickened. Set aside to cool.

6. When the baklava are ready and piping hot, place the tray on a work surface and pour the syrup over them, making sure it penetrates every bit of them and runs between the gaps. Leave for at least 12 hours before eating. The baklava can be stored in an airtight container for up to a week.

CHOCOLATE AND MINT CARAMEL CAKE

SERVES 8–10

Every family needs a good chocolate cake recipe for special occasions, and this is mine, inspired by the Icebreaker chocolate and mint bars I enjoyed as a child. It has no flour in it, using beaten egg whites to give it a lift instead, so it may sink a little after coming out of the oven. Don't worry, no one will notice once you've added the topping.

275g caster sugar
Large handful of mint leaves, finely chopped
250g dark chocolate (70% cocoa solids), broken into pieces
125g unsalted butter, plus extra for greasing
6 free-range eggs (4 separated and 1 yolk saved for use in another recipe)
Flavourless oil e.g. groundnut

FOR THE TOPPING
400ml double cream
4 tbsp icing sugar
6–8 drops of peppermint extract

1. Preheat the oven to 180°C/Gas 4. Lightly grease a baking tray with a little groundnut oil. Lightly grease a 23cm springform cake tin and line the base with baking paper.

2. Pour 100g of the caster sugar into a large frying pan and place it over a medium heat, shaking the pan occasionally, but not stirring, to ensure it melts evenly. Once it has turned a deep golden colour, scatter it with the mint leaves and tip on to the prepared tray. Set aside to cool. When cold and firm, break half the caramel into pieces and place in a bowl. Using the end of a rolling pin, crush them into very small pieces and set aside. Break the remaining caramel into small shards and reserve for decoration.

3. Melt the chocolate in a bowl that fits snugly over a pan of gently simmering water. (The bowl must not actually touch the water.) Add the butter and stir until melted. Set aside to cool slightly.

4. Beat 2 whole eggs and 3 egg yolks with 75g of the caster sugar until thick, light and fluffy. Fold in the chocolate mixture, then fold in the crushed caramel.

5. In another bowl, whisk the egg whites into soft peaks, then add the remaining 100g caster sugar a little at a time until it is all incorporated. The mixture should be in stiff, glossy peaks that hold their shape.

6. Fold a spoonful of the whites into the chocolate mixture, then carefully fold in the rest of them. Spoon into the prepared tin and bake for 35–40 minutes, until the cake has risen and the centre is no longer wobbly. Set aside to cool in the tin. Don't worry if the middle sinks a little – this often happens with flourless cakes. When cold, transfer the cake to a serving plate.

7. To make the topping, put the cream into a bowl, sift the icing sugar over it and add the peppermint extract. Whisk together until the cream begins to thicken and just holds its shape – take care not to overwhip.

8. Spoon the topping over the surface of the cake, leaving a narrow border around the edge to make for neater cutting.

9. Scatter the reserved caramel shards on top and serve.

SALTED CARAMEL POPCORN

SERVES 4

This shows that there's no food that can't be given a bit of a makeover. Popcorn's become a part of our Friday movie night routine at home and the children have got older they've developed a taste for the slightly more grown-up flavour of salted caramel.

100g dried corn kernels
200g golden caster sugar
1 tsp flaked sea salt
25g salted butter
½ tsp bicarbonate of soda
Flavourless oil, e.g. groundnut, for greasing

1. Cook the corn according to the packet instructions. Discard any kernels that have not opened and set the rest aside.

2. Place the empty popcorn pan over a medium heat and add the sugar and salt. Heat until the mixture caramelises, swirling the pan rather than stirring, until the caramel is a mid-golden colour. Stir in the butter and cook gently for a further 30 seconds.

3. Lower the heat and carefully add the bicarbonate of soda: the mixture will bubble up. Stir until combined, then immediately remove from the heat, add the cooked popcorn and stir until it is well coated.

4. Tip the popcorn on to a greased baking tray and leave at room temperature to harden. Do not put the mixture in the fridge or it will become sticky. Once cooled and crisp, break any large chunks into small pieces and store in an airtight container.

MAKING CARAMEL

If you are not confident about making caramel, you may find it easier to avoid using a non-stick pan as the black coating makes it harder to see the colour of the caramel changing (you are looking for a rich copper colour). If you do burn caramel, you have to start again. There is no way of disguising the bitter taste.

KITCHEN
SUPPERS

THIS CHAPTER IS PROBABLY THE MOST IMPORTANT ONE IN THE BOOK BECAUSE IT IS AIMED AT THE VAST MAJORITY OF THE COOKING WE DO.

For most of us that's a casual supper for the whole family that can be put together with the minimum of fuss any night of the week. I've filled it with family favourites like fish and mushy peas, whole roast chicken, shepherd's pie – the kind of food Tana and I sit down to as often as we can with Megan, Jack, Holly and Tilly. Except, of course, I've added plenty of twists along the way because the secret to good cooking is to keep it fresh and exciting. It makes it more interesting for the cook and it makes it more interesting for their family. Every one is a winner. So the batter on the fish is perked up with ginger beer, the roast chicken is stuffed with garlicky chickpeas, the shepherd's pie has got a cheesy champ topping. There really is no dish that can't be given a new spin.

What we really want from day-to-day cooking is ease and economy. We want simple dishes that taste good and don't cost the earth. A Tuesday night when you're late back from work and the children still haven't done their homework is no time to be composing complicated dishes that need hours of preparation. But that doesn't mean you shouldn't make them the best you can.

To give yourself the best head start, always plan ahead, so you know exactly what you are cooking. In the restaurant world, we call this "menu planning" (at home you'll simply call it "deciding what to eat") and it is the secret of every well-run kitchen as it allows you to work to full capacity. Get this right and the ease and economy bit will automatically follow. I'll look at menus week by week, but even at home, it's useful to think of meals in blocks of two or three days. It's not just the obvious things like ensuring you have all the right ingredients, but more fundamentally it's about making sure you choose the kind of cooking you can cope with. Even in a professional kitchen, where we have the luxury of

large brigades of chefs, with dozens of starters, mains and desserts to get out, the menu choice is dictated by what we can achieve. We have to make sure the workload is spread over the different sections, cold starters, meat, fish etc. You have to make a similar calculation at home, albeit on a smaller scale. If you are catering for large numbers, go for something simple like a hotpot, which doesn't need any last-minute fussing over. If you have the luxury of some spare time during the day, go for something that can be made well ahead, like slow-roasted beef brisket. If time is short, try something quick like a risotto.

The other advantage of forward planning is that you can incorporate leftovers into subsequent meals. Roast lamb on a Sunday? It makes sense to plan a shepherd's pie on the Monday.

The other thing that stacks the odds in your favour is to start with the best, seasonal ingredients. But remember, that doesn't necessarily mean the most expensive – there'll be plenty of time for that in the next chapter about more show-stopping suppers. The key here is to buy non-premium cuts of meat or less popular fish, use vegetables in season (see chart overleaf), when they'll be cheaper and tastier, and cook with attitude, injecting as much flavour as possible. And to ensure you have the wherewithal to do them justice, make sure you have a well-stocked storecupboard and freezer.

STORECUPBOARD

What I'm looking for here is a range of ingredients that will allow me to take my cooking in different directions, so on top of the absolute basics such as olive oil, wine vinegar, sea salt and black pepper, I'd include things like English and French mustard, flour, cornflour, tinned tomatoes, tinned anchovies, tinned chickpeas, tinned kidney beans, soy sauce, Worcestershire sauce, spices (cinnamon, cumin, coriander, curry, paprika, five spice), caster and icing sugar, honey, oatmeal, mixed nuts, pulses and grains.

Back in the old days, almost all our carbohydrates came from potatoes and bread. Now we have so much more to choose from, each of which can add variety to the supper table: polenta, which is an Italian cornmeal made with dried maize (I use the instant variety at home as it is ready in ten minutes); couscous (again, use the instant variety); quinoa, barley and Puy lentils, which are all pretty much interchangeable but bring a different flavour and texture to a dish; long grain rice (Basmati out of preference), risotto rice (I like Carnaroli best) and, of course, pastas and noodles, which are not only essential to Italian and Chinese cooking, but can also be used to bulk out soups and casseroles.

FREEZER

Green vegetables such as broad beans and peas (even during their season, it is better to buy frozen than those tired 'fresh' pods you see on supermarket shelves); lots of chicken and vegetable stock (see the chapter on soups for details), frozen into convenient sizes; breadcrumbs, not just to coat fish or chicken, but to scatter over a macaroni cheese before baking or to make pangrattato (fried in oil with garlic, anchovies, parsley and chilli and tipped over pasta).

SEASONAL CHART

JANUARY. Brussels sprouts, cabbage, carrots, celeriac, celery, greens, Jerusalem artichokes, kale, leeks, onions, parsnips, potatoes, shallots, squash, swede, turnips.

FEBRUARY. Beetroot, broccoli, Brussels sprouts, cabbage, carrots, cauliflower, celeriac, chard, chicory, Jerusalem artichokes, kale, kohlrabi, leeks, onions, parsnips, potatoes, shallots, spring greens, swede.

MARCH. Beetroot, broccoli, carrots, cauliflower, celeriac, chicory, leeks, mint, radishes, sorrel, spring onions.

APRIL. Carrots, kale, radishes, spinach, watercress, wild garlic.

MAY. Asparagus, purple-sprouting broccoli, broad beans, cabbages, carrots, lettuce, new potatoes, radishes, spring onions.

JUNE. Artichokes, asparagus, aubergines, beetroot, broad beans, broccoli, cabbages, carrots, cauliflower, courgettes, cucumber, garlic, lettuce, onions, peas, peppers, potatoes, radishes, spinach, turnips.

JULY. Artichokes, beans, beetroot, broccoli, cabbages, carrots, cauliflower, cucumber, fennel, garlic, lettuce, onions, peas, potatoes, radishes, rocket, shallots, spinach, spring onions, turnips, watercress.

AUGUST. Artichokes, aubergines, beans (broad, French and runner), beetroot, broccoli, cabbages, carrots, cauliflower, courgettes, cucumber, fennel, garlic, leeks, lettuce, onions, peas, potatoes, pumpkins, radishes, rocket, shallots, spinach, squash, sweetcorn, tomatoes, turnips, watercress.

SEPTEMBER. Aubergines, beans (broad, French and runner), beetroot, broccoli, cabbages, carrots, cauliflower, courgettes, cucumber, fennel, garlic, kale, leeks, lettuce, onions, peas, potatoes, pumpkins, rocket, spinach, squash, swede, sweetcorn, tomatoes, turnips, watercress.

OCTOBER. Artichokes, aubergines, beans, beetroot, broccoli, Brussels sprouts, cabbage, carrots, cauliflower, celeriac, celery, courgettes, cucumber, fennel, garlic, kale, leeks, lettuce, onions, parsnips, potatoes, pumpkins, rocket, spinach, squash, swede, tomatoes, turnips.

NOVEMBER. Beetroot, purple-sprouting broccoli, Brussels sprouts, cabbage, carrots, cauliflower, garlic, Jerusalem artichokes, kale, leeks, lettuce, onions, parsnips, potatoes, spinach, squash, swede, turnips.

DECEMBER. Beetroot, Brussels sprouts, cabbage, carrots, cauliflower, garlic, Jerusalem artichokes, kale, leeks, onions, parsnips, potatoes, pumpkins, spinach, squash, swede, turnips.

GRIDDLED POLENTA WITH ROASTED
VINE TOMATOES AND GOAT'S CURD

BLOODY MARY LINGUINE

LAMB KOFTAS WITH MINT
AND YOGHURT DRESSING

BEETROOT HOUMOUS
WITH ZA'ATAR SPRINKLE

BUTTERMILK-FRIED CHICKEN

QUICK SWEET PICKLED CELERY

HOME-MADE FISH FINGERS

SAUSAGE AND CARAMELISED
RED ONION HOTPOT

POTATO AND BEETROOT GRATIN

SHEPHERD'S PIE WITH
CHEESE CHAMP TOPPING

BRAISED PEAS AND CARROTS
WITH MINT BUTTER

CHILLI-MINTED MUSHY PEAS

GINGER BEER-BATTERED FISH

BEEF STEW WITH MUSTARD
SUET DUMPLINGS

TWICE-BAKED BUBBLE
AND JACKET POTATOES

ROASTED BEETROOT
AND THYME RISOTTO

ROAST CHICKEN WITH CHICKPEA
STUFFING AND BIG GREEN SALAD

CRISPY ROAST DUCK WITH CHINESE
PANCAKES AND DIPPING SAUCE

HOISIN AND CUCUMBER SALAD

BARBECUE-STYLE SLOW-ROASTED
BEEF BRISKET

CRUNCHY LIGHT COLESLAW

SPICED SWEET POTATO WEDGES

GRIDDLED POLENTA WITH ROASTED VINE TOMATOES AND GOAT'S CURD

SERVES 4

This simple dish is ideal as an easy help-yourself supper (and makes a delicious brunch dish too). You can make the polenta a couple of days in advance and then just finish it off in the griddle pan as your tomatoes roast in the oven. A lovely salty goat's curd sets it off beautifully but you could just as easily use cream cheese or crème fraîche.

200g instant polenta
Large knob of butter
75g Parmesan cheese, grated
400g tomatoes on the vine
Olive oil
2 garlic cloves, peeled and crushed

Pinch of sugar
2 thyme sprigs, leaves only, roughly chopped
Balsamic vinegar
250g creamy goat's cheese or goat's curd
4 basil sprigs, leaves torn
Sea salt and freshly ground black pepper

1. Preheat the oven to its highest setting. Grease a 2cm deep baking dish or tray.

2. Cook the polenta according to the packet instructions. Once cooked, beat in the butter and Parmesan. Taste and adjust the seasoning as necessary, then pour into the prepared dish. Cover and chill until set, about 20–30 minutes.

3. Meanwhile, snip the tomatoes into small clusters still attached to the vine. Place them on a baking tray and prick each tomato with the point of a knife. Drizzle with olive oil, sprinkle over the garlic, sugar and thyme, and season with salt and pepper. Drizzle with a little balsamic vinegar, then roast for 10–12 minutes, or until the tomatoes are blistered and tender.

4. Once the polenta is chilled, turn it out of the dish and slice it into wedges. Place a griddle pan over a medium heat. Brush the polenta wedges on either side with olive oil, season and griddle until charred and warmed through. You'll find it easiest to turn the wedges using a fish slice or palette knife.

5. To serve, place a wedge of polenta on a serving plate, sit a cluster of tomatoes on top and spoon over any juices from the roasting pan. Top with quenelles or dollops of goat's cheese or curd. Drizzle with a little more balsamic vinegar and garnish with the torn basil leaves.

USING POLENTA
Polenta is to the Italians what mashed potato is to Britons, a delicious staple. It's a cornmeal made of dried maize which is cooked in boiling water. I always use the instant variety when cooking at home because it is ready in 10 minutes, and add a drizzle of oil to the cooking water to stop it from sticking. Whether served fresh, or chilled and then griddled, it makes a great accompaniment to grilled meats.

BLOODY MARY LINGUINE

SERVES 4

This makes an unusual starter or main and just shows how even the most familiar dishes – in this case pasta and tomato sauce – can be updated. Bloody Mary is one of my favourite drinks, so I thought, why not incorporate the same flavours on the plate? The alcohol all evaporates but it adds a richness to the sauce. As a real treat I sometimes serve this with the Grilled Lobster with Chilli, Garlic and Parsley Butter on page 222.

Olive oil, for frying
1 red onion, peeled and finely diced
1 garlic clove, peeled and crushed
1–2 tbsp Worcestershire sauce
1 tsp Tabasco sauce
½ tsp celery salt
1 tsp caster sugar
1 x 400g tin best-quality chopped tomatoes
50ml vodka
400g dried linguine

FOR THE TOPPING
Olive oil, for frying
Large handful of white breadcrumbs
1 tbsp finely chopped parsley
Sea salt and freshly ground black pepper

1. First make the topping. Place a small frying pan over a medium heat and add a dash of olive oil. When hot, fry the breadcrumbs with a pinch of salt and pepper until golden. Stir through the parsley, transfer to a bowl and set aside.

2. Place a large frying pan over a medium heat and add a dash of oil. When hot, sauté the onion with a pinch of salt and pepper until softened and turning light golden. Add the garlic and continue to sauté for 2 minutes. Season to taste with the Worcestershire and Tabasco sauces, the celery salt and a sprinkling of sugar.

3. Pour in the vodka to deglaze the pan, scraping up the bits from the bottom. Add the tomatoes, bring to a simmer and cook gently for 10–15 minutes, until reduced a little and flavourful. Add a little water if the sauce thickens too much.

4. Meanwhile, cook the linguine according to the packet instructions. When al dente, drain and add to the pan of sauce along with a little of the pasta water. Mix well, then divide between warm serving plates and top with the herby breadcrumbs. Serve immediately.

HOW TO MAKE SILKY PASTA SAUCES
Whenever you make a pasta dish with a sauce, always reserve a tablespoon or two of the pasta water and stir it in to make the sauce silky smooth.

LAMB KOFTAS WITH MINT AND YOGHURT DRESSING

SERVES 4

These spicy Middle Eastern meatballs make a great midweek supper either with a crisp green salad, or stuffed inside a warmed pitta bread with lettuce, cucumber and tomatoes. Either way, drizzle over plenty of mint and yoghurt dressing to counteract the spice of the koftas. My Beetroot Houmous with Za'atar Sprinkle also works well with this dish (page 173). Photograph overleaf.

Olive oil
1 onion, peeled and finely diced
2 garlic cloves, peeled and crushed
2 tsp cumin seeds, toasted and ground
Chilli flakes, to taste
500g minced lamb
2 tbsp chopped parsley leaves
2 tbsp chopped mint leaves
Sea salt and freshly ground black pepper

FOR THE DRESSING
Small bunch of mint, leaves only
½ tsp toasted cumin seeds
2–3 tbsp natural yoghurt
Freshly ground black pepper
1 tbsp lemon juice

HOW TO MAKE YOUR OWN LAMB MINCE
You can make your own mince in a food processor, using trimmed shoulder, belly or neck fillet. If you do not have a mincing attachment, use the sharp cutting blade, adding cubed meat in stages and using the pulse button. If you add too much meat, or set the processor on continuous speed, the meat will become mushy.

1. Place a small frying pan over a medium heat and add a dash of oil. When hot, sauté the onion and garlic until tender. Add the cumin seeds and chilli flakes and cook, stirring, for about 2 minutes. Set aside to cool slightly.

2. Put the lamb into a mixing bowl, add the onion mixture and chopped herbs along with a drizzle of olive oil and a pinch of salt and pepper. Mix well with your hands.

3. Roll the lamb mixture into pieces the size of golf balls and flatten them into patties about 1 cm thick. Place on a plate drizzled with a little oil, and drizzle the tops of the patties with more oil, ready for cooking. Cover and chill for about 10 minutes to firm up.

4. Meanwhile, make the dressing. Put the mint into a mortar and bash it with the pestle to bruise it. Add the remaining ingredients and mix well. Taste and adjust the seasoning as necessary, then transfer to a serving bowl.

5. Place a griddle pan over a medium high heat. When hot, griddle the koftas for 5–6 minutes, turning halfway through so that both sides are well browned.

6. Serve the koftas warm with the dressing on the side.

BEETROOT HOUMOUS
WITH ZA'ATAR SPRINKLE

SERVES 4–6

Houmous has become almost commonplace now – the staple of many a packed lunch or picnic basket – so here's a nice twist. The beetroot adds colour, of course, but also a lovely sweetness. Serve it with grilled meats, such as the Lamb Koftas with Mint and Yoghurt Dressing (page 172), or as a dip with crudités or maybe Saffron Flat Breads (page 73). Za'atar is a typically Lebanese spice mix of dried herbs, sumac and toasted sesame seeds. You can buy it in supermarkets, but it's much nicer when you make your own, as here. Photograph overleaf.

1 tbsp cumin seeds, toasted
250g cooked chickpeas
250g cooked beetroot, chopped
1 tbsp tahini paste
1 garlic clove, peeled and crushed
Juice of 1 lemon
1–2 tbsp olive oil
Sea salt and freshly ground black pepper
Toasted flatbreads or pitta breads, to serve

FOR THE ZA'ATAR SPRINKLE

1 tsp cumin seeds, toasted
1 tsp sesame seeds
1 tsp ground sumac
½ tbsp marjoram leaves

1. First, combine all the ingredients for the za'atar sprinkle and mix well. Set aside.

2. To make the houmous, grind the tablespoon of cumin seeds to a powder using a mortar and pestle.

3. Put the chickpeas, beetroot, tahini and garlic into a food processor along with the ground cumin seeds and whiz until smooth. Add a tablespoon of olive oil, half the lemon juice and a good pinch of salt and pepper and whiz again. Taste and adjust the seasoning (including the lemon juice and oil) as necessary. If the mixture seems a bit thick and sticky, loosen it with a tablespoon or so of water.

4. Serve the houmous dusted with the za'atar sprinkle, and offer toasted flatbreads or pitta bread alongside.

USING SPICES

Buy your spices whole and grind them as needed to ensure they stay fresh. Store them in airtight tins or jars in a cool, dark place.

LAMB KOFTAS WITH MINT AND
YOGHURT DRESSING (RECIPE PAGE 172)

BEETROOT HOUMOUS WITH
ZA'ATAR SPRINKLE (RECIPE PAGE 173)

BUTTERMILK-FRIED CHICKEN

SERVES 4

Traditional southern fried chicken is simply coated in seasoned flour and fried, but marinating the chicken in buttermilk first tenderises the meat and gives it a lovely tangy flavour. I don't know what the colonel puts in his secret blend of herbs and spices. I use smoked paprika, garlic and cayenne pepper, and I'll tell you, it knocks the socks off his version. This is lovely with my Quick Sweet Pickled Celery.

4 free-range chicken thighs
4 free-range chicken drumsticks
500ml buttermilk
Flavourless oil, e.g. sunflower or groundnut,
  for deep-frying
300g plain flour
1–2 tsp smoked paprika
½ tsp garlic powder
1–2 tsp cayenne pepper
Sea salt and freshly ground black pepper

1. Place the chicken in a bowl, add the buttermilk and a good pinch of salt and mix well. Cover with cling film and chill overnight, or for at least 30 minutes. Bring back to room temperature before cooking.

2. Once ready to cook, pour a 1.5cm depth of oil into a heavy-based sauté pan or hob-proof casserole dish. Place over a medium heat until the oil reaches 170°C or a cube of bread dropped into the oil sizzles and turns brown after 30 seconds.

3. Put the flour on a plate and mix with the spices and a pinch of salt and pepper. Remove the chicken pieces from the buttermilk, shaking off any excess, then dip in the flour, making sure all sides are coated.

4. Fry the chicken in a single layer (you might need to do it in batches), turning constantly for 25–30 minutes, until evenly golden. Drain on kitchen paper and serve warm.

QUICK SWEET PICKLED CELERY

SERVES 4–6 AS A SIDE DISH

This is a quick and easy pickle to cut through the richness of the Buttermilk-fried Chicken or to go with any cold meats and cheeses. You want the celery to keep its crunch so don't cook it too long. Leaving it sitting in the sweet and sour poaching liquor means it will still take on plenty of flavour. If you wanted, you could add other vegetables such as carrot ribbons and sliced radishes to make it more substantial.

½ head of celery, trimmed
100g caster sugar
100ml white wine vinegar
4–5 cloves
1 tbsp mustard seeds
6 black peppercorns
Sea salt

1. Separate the celery and cut each stick diagonally into slices about 1cm thick. Set aside in a large bowl.

2. Place a small pan over a medium heat and add all the remaining ingredients, including 50ml water and a pinch of salt. Bring to the boil, then reduce the heat and simmer and stir until the sugar and salt have dissolved. Taste and adjust the seasoning as necessary. You want a balance between sour and sweet. Allow to cool until warm.

3. Pour the pickling liquid over the celery and leave to cool completely before eating. If placed in a sterilised airtight jar (see tip below) and stored in the fridge, the pickle will keep for up to a month.

HOW TO STERILISE GLASS JARS
To sterilise jars, and their lids, wash them thoroughly and allow to dry on a clean tea towel. Preheat the oven to its lowest setting, then place the jars and lids on a tray and heat in the oven for 30 minutes.

HOME-MADE FISH FINGERS
SERVES 4

I grew up on white fish such as cod, but pollack is another wonderful fish, perfect in my home-made fish fingers. I'm using panko breadcrumbs here, which are flakier than other crumbs and give fried food a lighter coating that stays crispy for longer. Running the crumbs through with dill makes the fish fingers more aromatic and they look fantastic. Give me these and a chip butty (page 94) and I'm like a nine-year-old kid again.

500g white fish fillet, e.g. pollack, skinned
4 dill sprigs, leaves only
100g panko breadcrumbs
4 tbsp plain flour
2 free-range eggs, beaten
Sunflower oil, for frying
Knob of butter
Sea salt and freshly ground black pepper

1. Slice the fish into chunky fish finger shapes. Sprinkle lightly with salt, then cover and place in the fridge for 20–30 minutes to firm up.

2. Finely chop the dill and mix with the breadcrumbs in a shallow bowl. Put the flour into another shallow bowl and season with salt and pepper. Put the beaten eggs into a third bowl.

3. Using kitchen paper, rub any excess salt off the fish. Dust the fish pieces in flour and shake off any excess, then dip in the egg, making sure all the sides are coated. Allow any excess to drip off, then cover in the dill breadcrumbs.

4. Place a large heavy-based frying pan over a medium-high heat and add enough sunflower oil to lightly coat the bottom. When hot, shallow-fry the fish fingers on either side for 3 minutes. Add the butter towards the end of the cooking time to help the fish fingers crisp up and turn a deep golden colour.

5. Drain on kitchen paper if necessary and season with a pinch of sea salt before serving.

SAUSAGE AND CARAMELISED RED ONION HOTPOT

SERVES 4

Rich and sweet with wine and caramelised onions, this takes the humble hot pot to another level and would be just the thing to have gently warming in the oven after a fireworks display or a long winter walk. Serve with buttered cabbage and potatoes or my Potato and Beetroot Gratin (page 181).

Olive oil, for frying
8 best-quality pork sausages
2 red onions, peeled and finely sliced
2 knobs of butter
1 tbsp soft brown sugar
3 thyme sprigs, leaves only
150g button mushrooms, cleaned and quartered
2 tbsp aged balsamic vinegar
200ml red wine
200ml beef stock
Small handful of parsley, roughly chopped
Sea salt and freshly ground black pepper

1. Preheat the oven to 180°C/Gas 4. Place a large hob-proof casserole dish over a medium heat. Add a dash of oil and fry the sausages until coloured all over. Transfer to a plate and set aside.

2. Add the onions and a couple of knobs of butter to the empty casserole dish. Stir in the sugar and thyme, then cook for 10–15 minutes over a medium heat, stirring now and again until the onions are completely caramelised. Add the mushrooms, stir, and continue to cook for 5 minutes. Pour in the vinegar and cook for a further 5 minutes.

3. Add the cooked sausages and red wine to the dish, bring to the boil and bubble for 4–5 minutes to burn off the alcohol and reduce slightly. Add the stock, bring to the boil, then transfer to the oven for 18–20 minutes uncovered until the sausages are cooked through and the sauce is thick. Sprinkle the finished dish with parsley and serve.

POTATO AND BEETROOT GRATIN
SERVES 4

This is a lovely twist on the classic gratin dauphinois, in which layered potato and beetroot is gently cooked in garlicky cream. I prefer to use waxy potatoes as they keep their shape better but whatever you use, cut them as thinly as possible, ideally in a food processor or mandoline. The beetroot should be cut thicker because it has already been cooked.

1 garlic clove, peeled and halved
Butter, for greasing
750g potatoes, peeled
500g cooked beetroot, peeled
500ml double cream
Sea salt and freshly ground black pepper

1. Preheat the oven to 180°C/Gas 4. Rub the inside of a 26 x 18cm baking dish with the cut sides of the garlic, then grease it with butter.

2. Slice the potatoes very thinly. Cut the beetroot into slices about 5mm thick. Heat the cream gently over a medium heat until hot.

3. Layer one-third of the potatoes into the prepared dish (save the best-looking pieces for the top). Cover with half the beetroot slices and season with salt and pepper. Repeat before finishing with a last layer of neatly arranged potatoes and season again.

4. Pour the hot cream over the dish and bake for 1 hour, or until the potatoes are completely tender. If the top seems to be browning too quickly towards the end of the cooking time, cover it with foil. Serve warm.

HOW TO COOK BEETROOT
Wrap the beetroots and a good sprinkling of salt in foil and cook them at 180°C/Gas 4 for about an hour, or until they feel soft when pierced with a skewer. Leave them to cool a little before peeling.

SHEPHERD'S PIE WITH CHEESE CHAMP TOPPING

SERVES 6

If I had to choose an all-time favourite family recipe, it would be this. My mum made the best shepherd's pie; the only complaint she ever got was that there wasn't enough. The secret is in browning the mince properly. Remember: no colour, no flavour. Accompany with Braised Peas and Carrots with Mint Butter (page 184).

Olive oil, for frying
1kg minced lamb
2 garlic cloves, peeled and finely chopped
1 onion, peeled and diced
2 leeks, trimmed, halved lengthways and finely sliced
1–2 tbsp Worcestershire sauce
1 tbsp tomato purée
100ml red wine
250ml chicken stock
2 rosemary sprigs, leaves only, chopped
Sea salt and freshly ground black pepper

FOR THE TOPPING

750g potatoes, e.g. Maris Piper, peeled and cut into chunks
50g butter
3 spring onions, trimmed and finely chopped
100g Cheddar cheese, grated
50–100ml milk (optional)

HOW TO CRISP UP MASHED POTATO

Whenever you need to crisp up mashed potato, run the tines of a fork over the potato to form little ridges then put the potato in the oven and bake at 180ºC/Gas 4 until golden. The ridges will help the potato to brown.

1. Preheat the oven to 180°C/Gas 4. Place a large, wide frying pan or hob-proof casserole dish over a medium-high heat. Add a dash of oil and fry the mince in batches, seasoning each lot, until well browned. Add the garlic for the last 2 minutes. Transfer to a plate.

2. Put a little more oil in the same pan and cook the onion and leeks over a medium heat for 5–7 minutes, until completely softened. Add Worcestershire sauce to taste, then stir in the tomato purée.

3. Return the mince to the pan and stir well. Pour in the wine, scraping up any bits from the bottom. Bubble for a couple of minutes to burn off the alcohol, then add the stock and bring to the boil. Reduce to a simmer, then add the rosemary and adjust the seasoning as necessary. Cook gently for 10–15 minutes, until the sauce has reduced slightly and the flavours are well combined. Set aside to cool.

4. Meanwhile, prepare the topping. Boil the potatoes until tender, then drain and mash until smooth. Mix in the butter and seasoning, then add the spring onions and three-quarters of the cheese and mix again. Taste and adjust the seasoning as necessary. If the mash is too dry add a splash of milk to loosen.

5. Put the lamb mixture into a 28 x 22cm baking dish and top with the mashed potato. Sprinkle with the remaining cheese and a little salt and pepper. Bake for 15–20 minutes or until the potato is golden brown and the meat is bubbling underneath, and serve.

BRAISED PEAS AND CARROTS WITH MINT BUTTER
SERVES 4

What else do you serve with Shepherd's Pie (page 182) but peas and carrots? But not just any old peas and carrots. I like to cook them in butter and stock to bring out their natural sweetness, and then top them off with minted butter. Photograph on previous page.

Knob of butter
250g baby carrots, cleaned and trimmed
300ml chicken or vegetable stock
200g frozen peas
Sea salt and freshly ground black pepper

FOR THE MINT BUTTER
100g butter, at room temperature
6 mint sprigs, leaves only, finely chopped

1. First make the mint butter. Put the ingredients for it into a bowl, add a few twists of pepper and mix well. Wrap in cling film and roll into a sausage shape. Chill until required.

2. Put a large knob of butter in a heavy-based sauté pan and place over a medium heat. When melted, add the carrots, toss well and add some salt and pepper. Pour in the stock, cover the pan with a lid and cook gently for 6–7 minutes.

3. Add the peas to the pan (plus a little extra stock if needed) and continue to cook for 3–4 minutes, until the peas are cooked through and the carrots are tender. Taste and adjust the seasoning as necessary.

4. Transfer the peas and carrots to a serving dish. Unwrap the mint butter, slice into discs and place a few on top of the veg. (Any leftover butter can be rewrapped and stored in the fridge for up to a week.) Serve immediately.

CHILLI-MINTED MUSHY PEAS

SERVES 4

Traditionally made with marrowfat peas, here
I am using the fresher garden peas, lightly crushed
with a potato masher or the back of a fork.
Continuing the spice theme, I've added a little chilli
to these – plus, of course, plenty of butter and mint.
Perfect with Ginger Beer-Battered fish (page 186).
Photograph overleaf.

Olive oil, for frying
Butter
1 banana shallot, peeled and finely diced
1 red chilli, finely chopped
1 garlic clove, peeled and crushed
400g frozen garden peas
4 mint sprigs
Sea salt and freshly ground black pepper

1. Place a heavy-based frying pan over a medium heat
and add a dash of oil and a knob of butter. When hot,
add the shallot and chilli and sauté for 2–3 minutes
before adding the garlic and a pinch of salt. Sauté
gently for 6–7 minutes, until completely soft.

2. Meanwhile, bring a large pan of water to the boil.
Add the peas, a pinch of salt and 2 mint sprigs and
cook until tender. Drain, discarding the mint.

3. Add the peas to the pan of shallot mixture. Mix well,
then roughly mash with a potato masher. Taste and
adjust the seasoning as necessary.

4. Finely shred the remaining mint leaves, mix
through the peas and serve.

GINGER BEER-BATTERED FISH

SERVES 4

Fish and chips with peas has got to be the ultimate comfort food, but I don't think you'll find my twist down at your local chippie. Adding a carbonated liquid such as lager or sparkling water to flour is a common way of creating a lighter, more aerated batter and the spice in ginger beer gives it an extra edge. Use an artisan ginger beer if you can, which will be less sweet and have more of a kick. Alternatively add a pinch of ground ginger along with the cayenne pepper. Serve with Chilli-Minted Mushy Peas (page 185).

4 meaty fillets of sustainable white fish, trimmed
    (cod, pollock, haddock or coley will all work
    equally well)
Flavourless oil, e.g. groundnut, for frying
Sea salt and freshly ground black pepper

FOR THE BATTER
225g plain flour, plus extra for dusting
2 tsp baking powder
Pinch of cayenne pepper
1 tbsp flavourless oil, e.g. groundnut
300ml ginger beer

HOW TO CHOOSE FISH
Whichever fish you use, make sure it is certified by the Marine Stewardship Council. It's essential that we manage marine resources carefully and the most powerful way of doing that is by making the right buying choices.

1. Place the fish on a plate and season with salt and pepper. Cover with cling film and chill for 10 minutes while you make the batter.

2. Sift the flour into a bowl and add the baking powder, cayenne pepper, a decent pinch of salt and a little black pepper. Add the oil and ginger beer, stirring as you do so, until the mixture has the consistency of thick double cream. Leave to stand for 30 minutes.

3. Pour a one-third depth of oil in a large, deep saucepan. Place over a medium heat until the temperature reaches 160°C, or a dollop of batter spooned into the oil rises immediately to the surface and bubbles form around the outside.

4. Place a handful of flour on a plate, season with salt and pepper and coat the fish in it, shaking off any excess. Give the batter a stir, dip the fish in it, allowing any excess to drip off, then fry for 3–5 minutes (depending on the thickness of the fish), until the batter is dark golden and crisp. Lift out with a slotted spoon, drain on kitchen paper and season with a pinch of salt. Keep warm while you cook the remaining fish in the same way.

5. Serve the fish warm with the Chilli-Minted Mushy Peas on the side, if using.

BEEF STEW WITH MUSTARD SUET DUMPLINGS

SERVES 4

This recipe showcases British cooking at its best: beautiful beef slow-cooked in beer and topped with light, fluffy dumplings. It's quite beautiful and just the sort of recipe everyone should have in their repertoire. You could equally use red wine instead of beer if you like, and the dumplings aren't essential, but I do urge you to give them a try. Serve with buttery carrots and greens or with my Twice-Baked Bubble and Squeak Jacket Potatoes (page 190).

700g braising beef, cut into chunks
2 tbsp plain flour, for dusting
Olive oil, for frying
2 carrots, peeled and cut into thick slices
150g pearl onions or baby shallots, peeled and trimmed
4 garlic cloves, bashed
4 thyme sprigs
3 bay leaves
500ml beer or ale
2–3 tsp tomato purée
300ml beef or chicken stock
Sea salt and freshly ground black pepper

FOR THE DUMPLINGS
125g self-raising flour, plus a little extra for dusting
75g suet
1 tbsp wholegrain mustard

1. Preheat the oven to 150°C/Gas 2.

2. Season the beef with salt and pepper, and dust in the flour. Place a large hob-proof casserole dish over a medium heat and add a dash of oil. When hot, brown the beef (in batches if necessary) until coloured on all sides.

3. Add the carrots, onions, garlic and herbs, stirring over a medium heat for 2–3 minutes.

4. Pour in the beer to deglaze the pan, scraping up the bits from the bottom. Boil for 2–3 minutes, then stir in the tomato purée. Add the stock and bring to a simmer. Mix well, then cover with a lid placing it very slightly askew to allow some steam to escape. Place in the oven for 2½ hours, until the beef is really tender.

5. Meanwhile, make the dumplings. Place the flour and suet in a bowl, add a pinch of salt and pepper, then the mustard. Mix to combine, then add a touch of warm water and bring it all together to form a thick dough. (Add a little extra flour if the mixture becomes too wet.)

6. With floured hands, roll the dough into 8–12 balls (depending on the size you prefer).

7. Remove the stew from the oven and increase the temperature to 180°C/Gas 4. Place the dumplings in the stew, replace the lid and cook for a further 20–25 minutes, until the dumplings have grown in size and are soft and tender. (If you prefer your dumplings to have a crisp top, don't cover the dish when returning it to the oven.) Cool slightly before serving.

TWICE-BAKED BUBBLE AND SQUEAK JACKET POTATOES

SERVES 4

These delicious potatoes make a great veggie main course in their own right, perhaps with a little cheese grated over, but are also a great side accompaniment to a casserole such as the Beef Stew with Mustard Suet Dumplings (page 188). I often make mash, as here, by baking rather than boiling potatoes as it results in a fluffier, more potato-y flavour. And the joy of this recipe is that you don't waste the skins. Photograph on previous page.

4 baking potatoes
¾ head of Savoy cabbage, finely shredded
3–4 knobs of butter
Sea salt and freshly ground black pepper

1. Preheat the oven to 180°C/Gas 4.

2. Wash and dry the potatoes and bake in the oven for 1 hour, until cooked through and crisp on the outside.

3. Meanwhile, sauté the cabbage in a little butter and a dash of water until tender. Season with salt and pepper and drain off any excess moisture.

4. Slice the baked potatoes in half. Scoop out the flesh and transfer it to a mixing bowl. Mash in a couple of knobs of butter with a fork. Add the cabbage, mix well, then taste and adjust the seasoning as necessary. You might also need another knob of butter, depending on the kind of potato used.

5. Spoon the mashed potato back into the empty shells – it will come above the edges, which is good – and place on a baking tray. Return to the oven for 10–15 minutes, until the tops are golden and crisping. Serve straight away.

ROASTED BEETROOT
AND THYME RISOTTO
SERVES 4

Risottos have a tricky reputation, but they are actually very straightforward. You do need to put in the arm work, though, stirring continuously as the rice cooks. Beetroot is a wonderful root vegetable so please don't let childhood memories of the acidic pickled stuff put you off. It has a lovely sweet, earthy flavour and will stain the risotto a glorious purple colour. A perfect dish for non-meat eaters (don't forget, vegetarian Parmesan is readily available).

500g beetroot, peeled and chopped into chunks
Olive oil, for roasting
Pinch of sugar
Dash of balsamic vinegar
Sea salt and freshly ground black pepper

FOR THE RISOTTO
Extra virgin olive oil
2 banana shallots, peeled, halved lengthways and
  finely sliced
2 garlic cloves, peeled and finely sliced
4 thyme sprigs, leaves only
250g risotto rice e.g Arborio
150ml red wine
800ml hot vegetable stock
50g butter
75g Parmesan cheese, grated

HOW TO MAKE THE PERFECT RISOTTO
The key is not to flood the rice with the stock, adding it a little at a time so that you are in control. The final addition of butter and parmesan – the mantecato as the Italians call it – is another essential part of the process. Add them both, give the risotto a gentle stir and put the lid back on for a few minutes to allow the rice to absorb the rich flavours.

1. Preheat the oven to 180°C/Gas 4. Place the beetroot in a roasting tin, toss with a good glug of olive oil, the sugar, salt and pepper and the balsamic vinegar. Roast for 30 minutes, then add a dash of balsamic, stir and cook for a further 10 minutes, until tender.

2. Meanwhile make the risotto. Place a wide heavy-based saucepan over a medium heat and add a glug of olive oil. When hot, add the shallots and garlic, season with salt and pepper and sauté gently until softened but not browning. Stir in the thyme, then pour in the rice and stir until the grains begin to change colour.

3. Pour in the wine to deglaze the pan, scraping up the bits from the bottom. Continue stirring for 2–3 minutes, until the rice has absorbed the wine. Add a ladleful of hot stock and stir until absorbed. Repeat this process until you the rice is just cooked and has a rich, creamy consistency.

4. Add two-thirds of the tender beetroot chunks to the risotto and stir through.

5. Turn off the heat and stir in the butter and three-quarters of the Parmesan. Taste and adjust the seasoning as necessary. To serve, dot with the remaining beetroot, sprinkle with the remaining Parmesan and drizzle with a little olive oil.

ROAST CHICKEN WITH CHICKPEA STUFFING AND BIG GREEN SALAD

SERVES 4–6

This is the way I used to eat roast chicken in France. By slipping a beautiful tarragon butter under the skin, you not only keep the breast moist, but all that flavour gets absorbed by the chickpea stuffing as well. Take the stuffing out after cooking and mix in the cooked garlic and some of the vinaigrette and – I guarantee it – those will be the tastiest chickpeas you've ever had.

1 large free-range corn-fed chicken (about 2kg), giblets removed
Small bunch of tarragon, leaves roughly chopped
200g butter, at room temperature
3 heads of garlic, halved horizontally
Olive oil, for drizzling
Sea salt and freshly ground black pepper

FOR THE STUFFING
1 x 400g tin cooked chickpeas, drained and rinsed
2 red chillies, sliced
1 lemon, zested
3 thyme sprigs, leaves only
Olive oil

FOR THE SALAD
1 butter lettuce, washed
1 lollo rosso lettuce, washed
100g baby spinach
1 ripe avocado, peeled, stoned and chopped

FOR THE DRESSING
1 tbsp balsamic vinegar
1 tbsp Dijon mustard
1 tbsp runny honey
4–6 tbsp extra virgin olive oil

1. Preheat the oven to 200°C/Gas 6. Season the inside of the chicken. Place the tarragon and butter in a bowl and beat until combined. Season with salt and pepper. Loosen the skin over both chicken breasts by gently pushing your fingers underneath it. Now push the tarragon butter under the loosened skin so that it covers the whole crown.

2. To make the stuffing, put the chickpeas into a bowl, season and add the chillies, lemon zest, thyme leaves and a dash of olive oil. Mix well. Spoon the chickpea mixture inside the chicken cavity and place the whole lemon at the entrance.

3. Place the garlic heads, cut side down, in a roasting tin. Put the chicken on top and drizzle with olive oil. Season the outside of the chicken with salt and pepper and roast for 10–15 minutes, until turning golden and beginning to crisp up. Reduce the heat to 180°C/Gas 4 and continue roasting for 1¼–1½ hours, until cooked through and golden all over.

4. Extract the lemon from the cavity of the bird and spoon the stuffing into a large bowl. Place the chicken on a warm platter, cover loosely with foil and set aside to rest for 10–15 minutes.

5. Meanwhile, separate all the lettuce leaves and tear any really large ones into pieces. Place in a salad bowl along with the spinach and avocado.

6. Put all the dressing ingredients except the oil into a bowl and whisk well. Add a pinch of salt and pepper, then add the oil and mix until emulsified. Set aside.

7. Spoon the garlic out of the pan and squeeze the pulp into a sieve placed over the bowl of stuffing. Slice the roasted lemon in half and squeeze the juice over the garlic. Push the garlic and juice through the sieve with the back of a spoon. Mash the entire contents of the bowl with a potato masher, then add 1 tablespoon of the dressing. Mix well, then transfer to a serving bowl and drizzle with a little extra olive oil.

8. Add 2 tablespoons of the dressing to the salad, then toss, taste and adjust the seasoning as necessary, adding a little more dressing if needed. (Any leftover dressing can be stored in a screwtop jar in the fridge.) Serve immediately alongside the roast chicken and stuffing.

CRISPY ROAST DUCK WITH CHINESE PANCAKES AND DIPPING SAUCE

SERVES 4–6

This is absolutely my favourite kind of food for a simple, help-yourself supper. Although the duck needs a long time in the oven, you really can put it in and forget about it, and it will happily sit in there a bit longer if you're not ready. Then you simply pull it apart with a fork, heat the pancakes in the microwave and leave everyone to tuck in. Add some chilli flakes to the dipping sauce if you like it hot or, if you are feeling lazy, substitute it for more of the shop-bought hoisin sauce I use in the accompanying Hoisin and Cucumber Salad (page 195). Photograph overleaf.

1 duck
4 tbsp Chinese five-spice powder
4 star anise
2 garlic cloves, bashed
4cm piece of fresh root ginger, peeled and roughly sliced
4 spring onions, trimmed and cut in half
20 Chinese pancakes
Sea salt and freshly ground black pepper

FOR THE DIPPING SAUCE
Groundnut oil, for frying
2 garlic cloves, peeled and chopped
3–4 tbsp black bean sauce
2 tsp rice vinegar
1–2 tbsp soy sauce
½ –1 tbsp runny honey

1. Preheat the oven to 160°C/Gas 3.

2. Cut off and discard the flap of fat that hangs over the entrance to the duck's body cavity. Pat the inside of the cavity with kitchen paper, then season with salt and pepper. Rub the entire outside of the duck with the five-spice powder, massaging it into the skin. Put the star anise, garlic, ginger and spring onions into the cavity.

3. Place the duck on a rack set over a roasting tin and roast for 160°C/Gas 3 for 1 hour then turn the oven down to 140°C/Gas 1 and cook for a further 2½–3 hours, until the flesh is really tender and the skin crisp.

4. Meanwhile, make the dipping sauce. Place a small saucepan over a medium heat and add a dash of oil. When hot, fry the garlic until tender but not colouring. Add 3 tablespoons of the black bean sauce, the vinegar, 1 tablespoon soy sauce and ½ tablespoon honey. Mix well and cook over a low heat for 3–4 minutes, until warmed through. Taste and adjust the flavours as necessary – you might need a little more soy sauce or honey, depending on the saltiness or sweetness of the black bean sauce you are using. Transfer to dipping bowls.

5. Once the duck is cooked, transfer to a plate, cover loosely with foil and set aside to rest for 15 minutes.

6. When the duck has rested, heat the pancakes according to the packet instructions. Meanwhile, flake the meat off the duck by pulling it apart with two forks. Serve with the dipping sauce and the warm pancakes.

HOW TO MINIMISE FAT WHEN COOKING DUCK
Duck is less meaty than chicken but its rich flavour means it goes further. Set it on a trivet when roasting as a lot of the fat will render off as it cooks.

HOISIN AND CUCUMBER SALAD
SERVES 4

Duck pancakes are always served with cucumber and spring onion in restaurants. For some reason they always cut them into small matchsticks, but I always think they look much more impressive cut into ribbons, as here. I also like to add gem lettuce to make the salad go further. Photograph overleaf.

1 large cucumber
4 spring onions, trimmed
2 baby gem lettuce

FOR THE DRESSING
2 tbsp hoisin sauce
2cm piece of fresh root ginger, peeled and grated
½ tbsp soy sauce
½–1 tbsp rice vinegar, or to taste
Dash of sesame oil

1. Trim the ends off the cucumber and cut in half lengthways. Scoop out the seeds with a teaspoon. Using a vegetable peeler, cut the cucumber into long, thin ribbons. Place in a salad bowl.

2. Thinly julienne the spring onions (see tip below) and add to the cucumber. Shred the lettuce lengthways into long thin strips and mix with the cucumber and onions.

3. To make the dressing, put all the ingredients into a bowl with 2 tablespoons cold water. Mix well, taste and adjust the seasoning as necessary. Pour over the salad, toss well and serve immediately.

HOW TO CUT JULIENNE STRIPS
Julienne are fine strips about the size of matchsticks. To make them, peel and core your ingredient, as necessary, then cut in half or into quarters. Place flat side down on a work surface and cut into slices about 5mm thick. Cut these slices into matchstick-sized pieces.

**HOISIN AND CUCUMBER SALAD
(RECIPE PAGE 195)**

CRISPY ROAST DUCK WITH CHINESE
PANCAKES AND DIPPING SAUCE
(RECIPE PAGE 194)

BARBECUE-STYLE SLOW-ROASTED BEEF BRISKET

SERVES 6

Like the roast duck, this is another slow and easy dish which amply rewards a little forward planning. You simply rub the beef in spices and seal it over a high heat, caramelise some onions and then leave it to take care of itself in the oven for three or four hours. It's amazing how much of a barbecue flavour it takes on without you having to go anywhere near the charcoal. Serve with Crunchy Light Coleslaw and Spiced Sweet Potato Wedges (both page 199) for a taste of the Deep South. Photograph overleaf.

1kg beef brisket, excess fat trimmed off to leave
  just 1cm
2 onions, peeled and sliced
6 bay leaves
2 tbsp light brown or muscovado sugar
1 tbsp tomato purée
1 x 300ml bottle lager
350ml beef stock
1 tbsp cider vinegar (optional)

FOR THE RUB
2 tsp cayenne pepper
2 tsp mustard powder
2 tsp freshly ground cumin seeds
2 tsp celery seeds
Sea salt and freshly ground black pepper

1. Preheat the oven to 140°C/Gas 1.

2. First make the rub. Combine all the ingredients for it in a bowl and mix well. Rub the mixture all over the brisket.

3. Place a roasting tin on the hob and add a glug of oil. When hot, seal the beef on all sides until coloured. Transfer to a plate and set aside.

4. Add the onions, bay leaves and sugar to the roasting tin along with a pinch of salt and pepper, and cook over a medium heat until the onions are soft and caramelised. Add the tomato purée and stir for 1 minute. Pour in the beer to deglaze the pan, scraping up the bits stuck to the bottom.

5. Put the brisket back into the pan on top of the onions and pour over the beef stock. Bring to the boil, then cover tightly with foil and transfer to the oven for 3–3½ hours, until tender. Baste the brisket every now and again so that the meat is nicely glazed in the pan juices.

6. Transfer the joint to a serving dish, cover loosely with foil and set aside to rest for 15–20 minutes.

7. Meanwhile, place the roasting tin over a medium-high heat to reduce the sauce adding the cider vinegar if using. Pour any of the resting meat juices into the tin as you do so.

8. To serve, slice the brisket and spoon the sauce over it.

CRUNCHY LIGHT COLESLAW

SERVES 6–8

Sometimes coleslaw made with mayonnaise can be too heavy, especially if, as here, we're teaming it with rich brisket. Keep it nice and light with a mustardy yoghurt dressing. The aim here is to provide some crunch to go with the succulent brisket, so dress the vegetables at the last minute so they are still crisp. Photograph overleaf.

¼ head of red cabbage, core and outer
   leaves removed
¼ head of white cabbage, core and outer leaves
   leaves removed
Bunch of chives, finely chopped

FOR THE DRESSING
200g natural yoghurt
1 tbsp wholegrain mustard
1–2 tsp cider vinegar
Sea salt and freshly ground black pepper

1. Finely shred the red and white cabbage. Place in a mixing bowl. Add the chives and mix well.

2. Combine all the dressing ingredients in a bowl, mix well and season to taste. Pour it over the vegetables, toss well and serve.

SPICED SWEET POTATO WEDGES

SERVES 4

With their creamy, fluffy orange flesh, sweet potatoes make a great alternative to the regular potato. I've never got the American thing of topping them with marshmallows, as they typically do at Thanksgiving, but cutting them into wedges and rubbing them in a ground spice mix works really well. Photograph overleaf.

1 tsp coriander seeds
1 tsp smoked paprika
½ tsp cayenne pepper
½ tsp dried oregano
1kg sweet potatoes
Olive oil, for drizzling
Sea salt and freshly ground black pepper

1. Preheat and oven to 200°C/Gas 6.

2. Toast the coriander seeds in a dry pan over a medium heat until aromatic. Transfer to a mortar and pound with a pestle until broken up. Add a decent pinch of salt, a couple of twists of pepper, the remaining spices and oregano. Mix well.

3. Cut the sweet potatoes lengthways into wedges about 2.5cm thick. Place them in a roasting tin, drizzle with oil and toss until coated. Sprinkle evenly with the spice mix and toss again.

4. Roast the wedges in the oven for 15 minutes, then turn with a fish slice and cook for a further 10–15 minutes, until tender.

HOW TO TOAST SPICES
Toasting spices in a dry pan for even just a few seconds enhances and draws out their fragrance. Be careful not to burn them or they will turn bitter and you'll taste it in the final dish.

SPICED SWEET POTATO WEDGES
(RECIPE PAGE 199)

**BARBECUE-STYLE SLOW-ROASTED
BEEF BRISKET (RECIPE PAGE 198)**

**CRUNCHY LIGHT COLESLAW
(RECIPE PAGE 199)**

FRIENDS
FOR
DINNER

THIS IS WHERE THE FUN HAPPENS, BECAUSE ULTIMATELY, IF YOU LOVE COOKING, WHAT YOU REALLY WANT IS AN APPRECIATIVE AUDIENCE SAT AROUND THE DINING ROOM TABLE.

Even after all these years working in Michelin-starred kitchens, I still get a huge buzz from that, knowing that all my hard work is being enjoyed by my friends. It's important to realise that I'm not trying to replicate the three-star treatment at home, though. I'm not here to prepare different hors d'oeuvres, to send out ornately plated up dishes cooked to order, different fish and meat courses, pre-dessert palate cleansers... You've got restaurants for all that. No, what I like to offer is more a spirit of hospitality, where my guests can see that I've gone to an effort, that I want to feed them well, but not so much that I'm stuck in the kitchen all evening.

I think home cooks sometimes get intimidated by the thought of cooking for a big crowd of people so they give up and serve shop-bought food instead. But, trust me, with a bit of planning and great recipes it's easy. Menu planning is crucial here. You have to be realistic about how much you can achieve and make things as easy as possible for yourself. If you are doing the whole three-course affair (which personally I don't think is always necessary in these more relaxed times) then make sure one course can be done well in advance – a soup or salad, for example. Maybe serve cheese instead of pudding (I always think a large block of one cheese looks more generous than small portions of several cheeses) or put some bars of good chocolate on the table and let guests help themselves over coffee. These aren't failures of hospitality, they are the signs of a confident host who knows that if they are relaxed, all their guests will be relaxed too.

So what are the best dishes for making a good impression? I think you can go three ways. First, and most obvious, is to throw some luxury at it. It gets expensive if you are cooking for a crowd, obviously, but a beautiful lobster tail or rib of beef will always turn a meal into a special occasion. A little truffle grated over a plate of buttery tagliatelle is so easy, but will make your guests feel special, especially if it is a white Alba truffle from Italy. If using a black Perigord truffle from France I'd be more likely to use it as a stuffing, along with some butter, between the skin and breast meat of a chicken or guinea fowl.

Alternatively, go for something that might not be that luxurious but makes an impact when you bring it to the table. I'd include large joints of meat such as a leg of lamb or a rolled belly of pork in this category, or maybe my whole Salt-crust Sea Bream (page 218), which has a real sense of theatre about it as you crack open the salt crust and all those wonderful smells waft out. Dishes like this are ideal for serving large numbers as they are as easy to make for four as they are for 12 – you just have to adjust the cooking time. It's nice to carve meat or fillet fish at the table, but if that makes you nervous by all means take it back to the kitchen to carve. Bring it back out on a large serving platter, though, so the effect isn't lost.

The third route is to offer an embarrassment of riches, almost a mini banquet, to underscore your generosity. I was really struck by how seriously they take family eating in Asia, where they all sit down together and put lots of dishes in the middle of the table for people to help themselves. I love that kind of entertaining. It's very social and relaxed and it's an approach we have adopted in our house too. There will be a bit more work to do beforehand, prepping several dishes, but the reward is a happy buzz as everyone tucks in. The Sticky Spiced Chicken Wings on page 228 are a good example of this kind of eating. On their own, they may seem a bit a simplistic, but add a dish of stir-fried green beans with soy and peanut dressing and a bowl of Thai rice and you've got an absolute feast.

SLOW-BRAISED BEEF CHEEKS
WITH PAPPARDELLE

CHICKEN FRICASSÉE

SAUTÉED POTATOES

HERBY BUTTER BEAN SALAD
WITH CRISPY PITTA BREAD

POMEGRANATE MOLASSES-MARINATED
SPATCHCOCK QUAIL

SALT-CRUST SEA BREAM

BRAISED LEEKS WITH HAZELNUTS

CHINESE BRAISED OXTAIL

RADISH SALAD

GRILLED LOBSTER WITH CHILLI,
GARLIC AND PARSLEY BUTTER

BEEF FILLET WITH SALSA VERDE

BAKED NEW POTATOES WITH
TRUFFLE AND PARMESAN

STICKY SPICED CHICKEN WINGS

STIR-FRIED GREEN BEANS WITH
SOY AND PEANUT DRESSING

THAI RICE WITH CURRY PASTE
AND GREEN HERBS

SLOW-COOKED SMOKY PULLED
PORK BUTT WITH CHIPOTLE MAYO

CRUSHED POTATOES WITH
SPRING ONIONS AND CHEESE

BROCCOLI SLAW

STUFFED RIB OF BEEF

HORSERADISH YORKSHIRE PUDDINGS

AROMATIC LAMB CHOPS
WITH MINTY YOGHURT

CHARGRILLED BROCCOLI AND
BULGUR SALAD

SLOW-BRAISED BEEF CHEEKS WITH PAPPARDELLE

SERVES 4–6

Every Italian family has their own version of the famous tomato and meat ragú, typically made with rabbit or wild boar. I'm using ox cheeks instead, which are cheap but flavoursome and well worthy of any dinner table. Don't skimp on that cooking time – it's the secret of the richly complex sauce which elevates this dish from its humble bolognaise cousin.

Olive oil, for frying
1kg beef cheeks or stewing beef
1 onion, peeled and roughly diced
2 garlic cloves, peeled and roughly crushed
1 bay leaf
400ml red wine
1 x 400g tin chopped tomatoes
500ml beef stock
500g dried pappardelle
Handful of parsley, finely chopped
Sea salt and freshly ground black pepper

1. Preheat the oven to 150°C/Gas 2.

2. Place a heavy-based hob-proof casserole dish over a high heat and add a dash of oil. Season the beef on both sides and brown all over in the hot pan. Transfer to a plate and set aside.

3. Add the onion, garlic and bay leaf to the empty pan and cook for a couple of minutes, until softened and colouring around the edges.

4. Return the meat to the pan. Add the wine to deglaze the pan, scraping up the bits from the bottom. Stir in the tomatoes and the beef stock, season with a little salt and pepper and bring to a simmer.

5. Cover the pan with a lid slightly askew to allow some steam to escape, and place in the oven for 3½–4 hours, until the meat is completely tender and the sauce rich and thick. Check the liquid level after 2 hours, topping it up with some water if necessary.

6. Cook the pappardelle in boiling salted water according to the packet instructions, until al dente. Drain and drizzle with olive oil and season with salt and pepper.

7. Place a ladleful of sauce in the bottom of a serving dish and top with the pasta. Finish with the beef, shredded if you like, in the sauce, and a sprinkling of parsley.

HOW TO COOK PASTA
Always use well-salted water to cook pasta because it is impossible to season later. The Italians always use 10g (2 teaspoons) salt for every litre of water. Adding olive oil to the cooking water is helpful, but if you really want to ensure that your pasta doesn't stick as it cooks, use plenty of water and twist the pan from side to side a few times to get the pasta swirling around just after you've put it in.

CHICKEN FRICASSÉE

SERVES 4

'Fricassée' is one of those old-fashioned terms which basically just means braised. Here I'm cooking a jointed chicken with smoked bacon, garlic and mushrooms before flambéing it in brandy and poaching it in a rich chicken stock. You could add some double cream towards the end if you wanted to enrich the sauce but, to be honest, made with a quality chicken, it is already my ultimate home-cooked French dinner, especially if when it is paired with the Sautéed Potatoes on page 214.

2 tablespoons olive oil
1 large free-range chicken, jointed into 8 pieces (2 drumsticks, 2 thighs, 2 breasts cut in half)
150g smoked bacon lardons
4 garlic cloves, peeled and bashed
150g chestnut mushrooms, halved
1 bay leaf
2 rosemary sprigs
2 thyme sprigs, leaves only
75ml brandy
450ml chicken stock
Small handful of parsley, chopped
Sea salt and freshly ground black pepper

1. Place a large heavy-based sauté pan over a medium heat and add the olive oil. Season the chicken, add to the hot pan and sauté for 3–4 minutes on one side, until golden. Turn the chicken, then add the lardons, garlic and mushrooms and mix well. Stir in the bay, rosemary and thyme.

2. Add the brandy and, very carefully, tilt the hot pan towards the lit gas to ignite the alcohol and flambé the chicken. This must be done cautiously because it will create a huge flame. Allow it to die down, then lower the heat slightly and simmer gently for 2–3 minutes.

3. Pour in the chicken stock and bring to a gentle simmer. Cook uncovered for 10 minutes, then cover and cook for a further 15–20 minutes, until all the chicken pieces are done. Transfer them to a plate, then increase the heat under the pan for a few minutes to reduce and slightly thicken the sauce. Return the chicken to the pan and spoon the sauce over it.

4. Before serving, discard the garlic, rosemary and bay leaf, and sprinkle with the chopped parsley.

HOW TO MAKE THE MOST OF HERBS
Fresh herbs are a great way to add maximum flavour on a low budget. Make them last longer by standing the stems in a glass of water. They'll keep this way for up to 2 weeks in the fridge.

SAUTÉED POTATOES
SERVES 4

The French didn't invent the fried potato, but they certainly know how to take it to another level. The shallots, garlic and herbs all add extra interest, but it's the goose fat that is the real star, producing burnished golden spuds. If you aren't already a convert, do use goose fat for the best roast potatoes too. Photograph on previous page.

5 waxy potatoes, e.g. Desirée, unpeeled and sliced
   ½ cm thick
1 tbsp goose fat
2 banana shallots, peeled and finely sliced
3 garlic cloves, peeled and finely sliced
2 rosemary sprigs
2 thyme sprigs
Sea salt and freshly ground black pepper

1. Parboil the potato slices in a pan of salted boiling water for 5–6 minutes. Drain and season with salt and pepper.

2. Place a large heavy-based frying pan over a medium heat and add the goose fat. When melted and hot, add the potatoes and fry for 1–2 minutes on either side, until beginning to brown. Add the shallots and garlic, season with salt and pepper, then add the herbs (you may need to do this in batches). Continue cooking until everything is nice and golden. Serve straight away.

HERBY BUTTER BEAN SALAD WITH CRISPY PITTA BREAD

SERVES 4

If you don't want teenagers, especially hungry boys, to turn up their noses at a salad, be sure to pack it full of carbohydrates to fill them up. This Lebanese-inspired salad includes both pitta bread and butter beans, which make a mellow counterpoint to the sharpness of the lemon juice, sumac (a citrus-flavoured crushed berry) and pomegranate seeds. Great for a summer picnic with grilled meats or with Pomegranate Molasses-Marinated Spatchcock Quail (page 216). Photograph overleaf.

2 large pitta breads
Olive oil
1 x 400g tin cooked butter beans, drained
200g radishes, trimmed and halved
2–4 spring onions, trimmed and finely chopped
1 cucumber, deseeded and sliced
4 ripe tomatoes, chopped
4 celery sticks, finely sliced
Small bunch of mint, leaves finely chopped
Bunch of parsley, roughly chopped
Seeds from 1 pomegranate
1 tbsp ground sumac
Juice of 1 lemon and zest of ½
Sea salt and freshly ground black pepper

1. Slice the pitta breads into strips and cut across them to make squares about 2 x 2cm. Heat a large heavy-based frying pan over a medium heat. Add a glug of oil and fry the cubes in a single layer (you might need to do this in batches) until dark golden and crisp. Drain on kitchen paper and season with salt.

2. Mix all the remaining ingredients together in a large serving bowl. Drizzle with olive oil and season to taste. Toss in the pitta cubes, mix through and serve immediately.

HOW TO MAXIMISE LEMON JUICE
To get the maximum amount of juice from a lemon or lime, roll it hard under your palm for a minute before juicing.

POMEGRANATE MOLASSES-MARINATED SPATCHCOCK QUAIL

SERVES 4

This recipe is full of Middle Eastern flavours. I love the combination of spices and sweetness from the pomegranate molasses. The longer you can leave the quail to marinate the better. Spatchcocking is a great way of preparing quail, poussin or chicken. By removing the back bone and flattening the birds along the breast bone you shorten the cooking time, making it ideal for grilling or barbecuing. Pair with Herby Butter Bean Salad with Crispy Pitta Bread (page 215).

1 tbsp cumin seeds
1 tsp coriander seeds
2 garlic cloves, crushed
Olive oil
6 tbsp pomegranate molasses
4 spatchcocked quail
Sea salt and freshly ground black pepper
Zest of 1 lemon, to serve

HOW TO MAKE POMEGRANATE MOLASSES
You can buy pomegranate molasses from delis, Middle Eastern shops and some supermarkets, but it is easy to make your own. Simply boil up a litre of pomegranate juice with 100g sugar and the juice of one lemon. Simmer for about an hour until syrupy. Once cooled, you can store it for up to a month in the fridge and add to marinades, dressings and tagines.

1. Place a small pan over a medium heat, add the cumin and coriander seeds with a pinch of salt and dry-fry for about 2 minutes, or until aromatic. Transfer to a mortar and pound with a pestle.

2. Add the garlic, 2 tablespoons olive oil and the pomegranate molasses to the mortar. Mix well, then taste and adjust the seasoning as necessary.

3. Season the quail and place in a single layer in a baking dish. Pour the marinade over them, ensuring that all parts are covered. Cover with cling film and marinate in the fridge for at least 30 minutes, and up to 24 hours.

4. Preheat the oven to 180°C/Gas 4.

5. Place a large ovenproof frying pan over a medium heat and add a dash of oil. When hot, put the quail into the pan, skin side down, and fry for 2–3 minutes, until sealed and lightly coloured. Turn and cook the other side for 2–3 minutes. Add 100ml water, then transfer the pan to the oven and cook for 12–15 minutes, until the quail are cooked through, dark golden and sticky.

6. Serve sprinkled with lemon zest.

SALT-CRUST SEA BREAM
SERVES 4

Cooking fish inside a salt crust is very traditional. The salt insulates the fish from the extremes of heat, ensuring it cooks evenly and seals in all the flavours and juices. It also makes for a dramatic centrepiece if you crack it open at the table. And no, the fish won't taste salty – the scales protect the flesh so it remains sweet and succulent. You can use this type of cooking for most types of fish, though it's not ideal for oily varieties such as salmon and mackerel.

2 sea bream (try gilthead, if possible), each about
    400–500g, gutted and cleaned, scales on
½ tsp fennel seeds
1 lemon, sliced
1.5–2kg fine sea salt
Sea salt and freshly ground black pepper

1. Preheat the oven to 180°C/Gas 4.

2. Season the stomach cavity of each fish, then sprinkle in the fennel seeds and arrange the lemon slices inside.

3. Mix the salt with about 100ml water until it starts to resemble wet snow. Place a 2cm layer of the salt mixture in a roasting tin and sit the fish on it top to tail. Cover them with the remaining salt, patting it down to make sure there are no gaps.

4. Place in the oven for 25 minutes, or until the fish are just cooked through and smell aromatic, and the salt has formed a hard crust.

5. Crack open the salt crust by hitting it with the back of a spoon, then carefully lift it off. Peel off any skin remaining on the fish. Using the edge of a spoon, run it down the middle of the flesh and gently push each fillet away from the bones: they should come away easily.

BRAISED LEEKS WITH HAZELNUTS

SERVES 4

This side dish is all about texture, with the sweet, soft leeks enhanced by the crunch of the toasted hazelnuts. The secret is to get good colour on the leeks before adding the liquid as it adds extra flavour. It would go really nicely with any fish dish, such as Salt-Crust Sea Bream (page 218).

Olive oil, for frying
4 leeks, white parts only, cut into pieces 4–5cm long
2–3 garlic cloves, bashed
3 thyme sprigs
Knob of butter
150ml white wine
50g blanched hazelnuts, toasted and roughly crushed or chopped
2 tbsp chopped parsley
Sea salt and freshly ground black pepper

1. Place a heavy-based sauté pan over a medium heat and add a dash of oil. When hot, add the leeks and some seasoning, then cook for 3–4 minutes, turning frequently, until they are a rich golden colour on at least two sides.

2. Add the garlic, thyme and butter. Once the butter has melted, add the wine and bring to the boil. Partially cover the pan, lower the heat and simmer gently for 12–15 minutes, until the leeks are tender but still holding their shape. If there is a lot of liquid, remove the lid for the last 5 minutes of cooking time in order to reduce it.

3. Transfer the braised leeks to a serving dish, sprinkle with the hazelnuts and parsley, and pour any cooking juices over the top.

HOW TO COOK LEEKS
Don't completely cover leeks when you cook them or the condensation will make them waterlogged and mushy. For best results, you want the steam to be able to escape.

CHINESE BRAISED OXTAIL
SERVES 4–6

A lot of Chinese cooking involves quick stir-frying over high heat, but they also have a long tradition of slow braises. The combination of melting oxtail and warming spice is wonderful on a winter's night. I like to serve this with buttered noodles and the Radish Salad.

2kg oxtail pieces, any lumps of fat trimmed off
Plain flour
Oil, for frying
4 garlic cloves, peeled and crushed
1 onion, peeled and diced
1 red chilli, sliced
1 fennel bulb, diced
4cm piece of fresh root ginger, peeled and sliced
4 tbsp soy sauce
1 tsp coriander seeds
4 whole star anise
4 tbsp Chinese rice wine or dry sherry
850ml chicken stock
Sea salt and freshly ground black pepper

1. Preheat the oven to 160°C/Gas 3. Dust the oxtail in flour, shaking off any excess, season with salt and pepper. Place a heavy-based hob-proof casserole dish on a medium heat and add a dash of oil. When hot, add the oxtail and crushed garlic, and fry on all sides until browned. It's best to do this in batches. Transfer the meat to a plate and set aside.

2. Add a little more oil to the pan. When hot, add the onion, chilli, fennel, ginger, soy sauce, coriander seeds and star anise. Sauté for a minute then add the rice wine vinegar and cook for a further 2 minutes before adding the meat back in to the pan.

3. Add the stock and bring to a simmer. Cover with a lid and place in the oven for 2½–3 hours, turning the oxtail pieces occasionally, until the meat is really tender. Serve with the sauce spooned over it.

RADISH SALAD
SERVES 4

Simplicity itself. Four ingredients – radishes, shallots, lemon and olive oil – which combine to produce far more than the sum of their parts. The freshness of the radishes is everything here as this dish is all about the crunch.

2 bunches of radishes, leaves on (about 400g in total)
1 banana shallot, peeled and very finely sliced
1 lemon
Olive oil, for drizzling
Sea salt and freshly ground black pepper

1. Separate the leaves from the radishes. Wash both really well and pat dry.

2. Slice half the radishes and place in a serving bowl. Trim the whole radishes and add to the bowl along with the leaves. Mix in the shallot, then dress the salad with lemon juice, a drizzle of olive oil and some seasoning.

HOW TO PREPARE RADISHES
Wash the radish leaves carefully as they can be very gritty. If the radish roots need perking up a little, place the sliced halves in iced water for ten minutes. This will make them slightly crisper.

GRILLED LOBSTER WITH CHILLI, GARLIC AND PARSLEY BUTTER

SERVES 4

Lobster is such a luxury, you really don't want to overcomplicate it. A simple dressing of chilli-spiked garlic butter is all you need to bring out its natural sweetness. You can, of course, buy ready prepared lobsters, but buying them live is the best way to guarantee freshness. My Bloody Mary Linguine (page 170) makes a great accompaniment.

4 x 600–700g lobsters, boiled for 6–7 minutes

FOR THE PARSLEY BUTTER
1 red chilli, deseeded if desired
1 garlic clove, peeled and finely chopped
3 tbsp finely chopped parsley
150g butter, softened
Sea salt and freshly ground black pepper

1. Put the chilli, a pinch of salt, the garlic and the parsley into a mortar and bash with a pestle until blended to a rough paste. Add the butter and mix thoroughly. Set aside.

2. Place a lobster on a chopping board, insert the tip of a heavy knife into the cross on the back of its head and cut down towards the tail to halve it lengthways, then cut through the head to create two equal halves. Discard the stomach sac and black intestinal tract along with any other gunk present. Snap off the big claws and use the back of your knife to crack the shell in places. Repeat this process with the other lobsters.

3. Spread the flavoured butter over the lobster flesh. Break off pieces of the shell on the claws and insert a little butter here as well. Then cover and chill for 10–20 minutes.

4. Place a griddle pan over a medium heat. When hot, place the lobsters on it, flesh side down, and cook for 3–4 minutes, to lightly char. Turn over and cook for a further 2 minutes with the claws, then serve.

HOW TO BOIL A LOBSTER
Every cook seems to have different opinions on the correct way to kill lobsters and other crustaceans and for the most humane way I recommend consulting the RSPCA website, which will show you which part of the lobster to cut before placing it in a large pan of salted, cold water and then bringing it to the boil.

BEEF FILLET
WITH SALSA VERDE
SERVES 6–8

The Rolls-Royce cut from the Rolls-Royce of meats: it would be sacrilege to mess around with this much. I like to serve fillet rare, so you can appreciate its almost buttery sweetness, but feel free to cook it a bit longer if you like. But please, not well done. That would be a travesty. Salsa verde is a sharp, punchy condiment from Italy that works particularly well with this cut. Team up with Baked New Potatoes with Truffle and Parmesan (page 225) for a real treat. Photograph overleaf.

Olive oil, for frying
1kg piece of beef fillet cut from the thick end
2 heads of garlic, halved horizontally
4 thyme sprigs
2 rosemary sprigs
Butter, for basting
Sea salt and freshly ground black pepper

FOR THE SALSA VERDE
5 anchovy fillets, reserve some of their oil
1½ tbsp capers
2 garlic cloves, peeled and crushed
1½ tbsp Dijon mustard
1½ tbsp sherry or red wine vinegar
Extra virgin olive oil
Bunch of parsley, leaves only
Small bunch of mint, leaves only
Freshly ground black pepper

HOW TO COOK BEEF FILLET
Because beef fillet is so lean, it can easily dry out. It's important to keep basting it, not just before it goes in the oven, but also once it comes out and is resting.

1. Preheat the oven to 200°C/Gas 6.

2. Place a heavy-based ovenproof frying pan over a medium heat and add a dash of olive oil. Season the beef all over, then brown in the pan on all sides for a minute or two. Add the garlic, thyme and rosemary and roll the beef around with the herbs. Add a couple of knobs of butter and, when melted, baste the beef in it. Transfer the pan to the oven and roast for 10–12 minutes (rare) or 15–17 (medium rare).

3. Meanwhile, make the salsa verde. Put the anchovies with a teaspoon of their oil, capers, garlic, a pinch of salt and the half the herbs, in a mortar and pound with a pestle until a paste has formed. Stir in the mustard and vinegar. Loosen with a little oil, then stir in the rest of the herbs. Mix well to your preferred consistency. Taste and adjust the seasoning as necessary.

4. Once the beef is cooked to your liking, baste it in the pan juices and transfer to a warm plate. Spoon over a couple of spoonfuls of salsa verde, cover loosely with foil and leave to rest for 10 minutes.

5. To serve, slice thickly and spoon the salsa verde alongside.

BAKED NEW POTATOES WITH TRUFFLE AND PARMESAN

SERVES 4

If you've already blown the budget on the Beef Fillet (page 224), why not go the whole hog and splash out on a truffle? As soon as it hits the heat of the potato, it will fill the room with its irresistible, pungent aroma. Black Perigord truffles from France are delicious, but best of all (and twice as expensive) are the white Alba variety from Italy. Photograph overleaf.

1kg baby new potatoes
Olive oil, for roasting
30g Parmesan cheese, grated
10g black truffle shavings (or white if you're
   feeling extravagant)
Sea salt and freshly ground black pepper

1. Preheat the oven to 180°C/Gas 4.

2. Place the potatoes in a roasting tin, toss in a little olive oil and season with salt and pepper. Roast for 30–35 minutes, until crisp on the outside and soft all the way through.

3. Place the potatoes in a serving bowl and toss with the Parmesan. Top with the truffle shavings and serve.

USING TRUFFLES
Truffles are equally good with scrambled eggs or silky pasta tossed in butter. Although part of the same fungus family as the mushroom, you should never cook them or they will lose their flavour. Simply grate or slice very thinly over your plate at the last minute.

**BAKED NEW POTATOES WITH TRUFFLE
AND PARMESAN (RECIPE PAGE 225)**

BEEF FILLET WITH SALSA VERDE (RECIPE PAGE 224)

STICKY SPICED CHICKEN WINGS

SERVES 4

Chicken isn't all about the breasts – the wings can be just as delicious, especially when coated in a spicy Asian marinade and roasted to sticky perfection. Combine them with Stir-Fried Green Beans and Thai Rice with Curry Paste and you have a perfect informal supper for friends. Photograph overleaf.

5 tbsp tamarind paste
2 tbsp flavourless oil, e.g. groundnut
2 tbsp palm or brown sugar
1 tbsp fish sauce
2 garlic cloves, peeled and finely chopped
1 tsp chilli powder or flakes
16–20 free-range chicken wings, depending on size, wing tips removed
4 spring onions, trimmed and sliced diagonally, to garnish

1. If using a block of tamarind, place it in a bowl with 2 tablespoons hot water to dissolve it. Remove any seeds, if necessary.

2. Put the tamarind paste in a large bowl with the oil, sugar, fish sauce, garlic and chilli and mix well. Add the wings and use your hands to toss them thoroughly in the mixture. Cover with cling film and marinate in the fridge overnight, or for at least 1 hour.

3. Preheat the oven to 180°C/Gas 4.

4. Line a roasting tin with foil (to make it easier to clean after cooking) and place the marinated wings in it. Roast for 25–35 minutes, until cooked through and sticky.

5. Serve the wings warm, garnished with the spring onions.

STIR–FRIED GREEN BEANS WITH SOY AND PEANUT DRESSING

SERVES 4

Although this requires some last minute stir-frying, you can part-cook the beans in boiling water well in advance, so they take literally four minutes to finish off. It's important to get the pan hot enough to blister the beans and give them some colour – if you have one now's the time to bring out your wok as it will help you to control the temperature more easily than a heavy pan. Photograph overleaf.

300g green beans, trimmed
2 tbsp crunchy peanut butter, or 3 tbsp peanuts blitzed in a food processor
1 tbsp soy sauce
½ tbsp rice vinegar
½ tbsp brown sugar
Flavourless oil, e.g. groundnut, for frying
2 garlic cloves, peeled and finely chopped
2 tbsp sesame seeds, toasted, to serve

1. Blanch the beans in salted boiling water for 2 minutes. Drain and refresh in cold iced water.

2. Put the peanut butter, soy sauce, vinegar and sugar in a bowl and mix together. Add 1–2 tablespoons hot water if the mixture is very thick. Stir until the sugar has dissolved.

3. Place a heavy-based frying pan or wok over a medium heat and add a dash of oil. Add the garlic and cook for 1 minute, until golden. Toss in the beans and cook for 2–3 minutes, until beginning to blister slightly on the outside.

4. Lower the heat, add the peanut dressing and stir well.

5. Transfer the beans to a serving bowl and sprinkle with the toasted sesame seeds.

THAI RICE WITH CURRY PASTE AND GREEN HERBS

SERVES 4

This is a staple dish throughout Thailand. If time is short, you can use best-quality shop-bought red or green curry paste, but it's so easy to make your own and the result will be far more vibrant. Photograph overleaf.

300g cooked jasmine or long-grain rice, preferably 1 day old or chilled for at least 4 hours
Flavourless oil, e.g. groundnut
Sea salt and freshly ground black pepper
Lime wedges, to serve

FOR THE CURRY PASTE
2 large green chillies
1 garlic clove, peeled and roughly chopped
1 lemongrass stalk, roughly chopped
2 lime leaves
3cm piece of fresh root ginger, peeled and chopped
Small bunch of coriander
1 shallot, peeled and chopped
Juice of 1 lime

1. First make the curry paste. Put all the ingredients for it into a food processor with 1–2 tablespoons oil plus a pinch of salt and pepper and blitz until smooth.

2. Place a large frying pan or wok over a medium-high heat and add a tablespoon of oil. When hot, add the curry paste and stir over the heat until aromatic (about 2 minutes).

3. Add the rice to the pan, stir well and cook for 4–5 minutes, until the rice is heated through. If necessary, add another dash of oil to prevent the rice from sticking to the pan. Taste and adjust the seasoning as you wish.

4. Transfer to a serving bowl and serve immediately with lime wedges.

HOW TO STIR-FRY
Tossing the contents of a pan with a smooth flick of the wrist doesn't just look good – it means you can stay in control and keep things cooking evenly. The secret is to push the pan away from you and sharply pull it back. Push away, pull back, push away, pull back. It will take a little practice, but it's a skill that's definitely worth perfecting.

THAI RICE WITH CURRY PASTE AND GREEN HERBS
(RECIPE PAGE 229)

**STICKY SPICED CHICKEN WINGS
(RECIPE PAGE 228)**

**STIR–FRIED GREEN BEANS WITH SOY AND
PEANUT DRESSING (RECIPE PAGE 228)**

SLOW-COOKED SMOKY PULLED PORK BUTT WITH CHIPOTLE MAYO

SERVES 8–10

The name might raise a snigger, but boy, wait until you taste this dish. The 'butt' is a cut from the middle of the pig's shoulder which, with long slow cooking, melts down to the sweetest, tenderest pork you'll ever taste. Served with a smoky mustard mayo, it's the ultimate American party food. All it needs are some Crushed Potatoes with Spring Onions and Cheese (page 233) and Broccoli Slaw (page 233). Photograph overleaf.

3 tbsp hot smoked paprika
2 tbsp demerara sugar
4 garlic cloves, peeled and crushed
4 thyme sprigs, leaves finely chopped,
   stems reserved
Olive oil
1 x 2–3kg pork butt (front middle shoulder),
   bone in, rind removed
4 onions, peeled and quartered
Sea salt and freshly ground black pepper
White baps, to serve

FOR THE CHIPOTLE MAYO
300g best-quality mayonnaise
1–2 tbsp chipotle paste (if unavailable, use 2 tsp
   smoked paprika)
1 tsp runny honey
1 tbsp wholegrain mustard

1. Preheat the oven to 140°C/Gas 1.

2. Mix the paprika, sugar, garlic and thyme leaves in a bowl. Season with salt and pepper, then add a little olive oil to create a paste. Rub the mixture all over the pork, massaging it into the meat. While it's absolutely fine to cook the pork at this point, you can also cover and chill it for up to 24 hours to absorb the spice rub.

3. Put the onions into a roasting tin, sprinkle with the thyme stalks and place the pork, fattiest side up, on top. Roast for 1 hour, then cover with foil and cook for a further 4–5 hours, until the meat is really tender and falling off the bone.

4. Meanwhile, make the chipotle mayo. Combine all the ingredients in a bowl, season with salt and pepper and mix well.

5. Once the pork is cooked, cover it loosely with foil and set aside to rest for up to 1 hour before pulling the meat away from the bone in chunks. Serve with the smoky mayo and baps alongside.

CRUSHED POTATOES WITH SPRING ONIONS AND CHEESE

SERVES 6–8

If you can't choose between baked and mashed potatoes, these offer the best of both worlds. Roughly crushed and topped with cornichons, spring onions and cheese, they make a no-nonsense accompaniment to my Slow-Cooked Smoky Pulled Pork Butt (page 232), or any other roast. Photograph overleaf.

1.25kg red-skinned potatoes, unpeeled (cut any large ones to the same size as the smaller ones)
30g of butter, optional
4 spring onions
100g cornichons or sweet pickled gherkins
175g Gruyère cheese, grated
Sea salt and freshly ground black pepper

1. Boil the potatoes in salted boiling water until tender.

2. Meanwhile, finely chop the spring onions on the diagonal and dice the cornichons.

3. Drain the potatoes and roughly crush them (still in their skins) with a potato masher. Add the butter if using. Stir in the spring onions and cornichons, then fold in the cheese. Taste and season as necessary, then serve.

HOW TO BOIL POTATOES WITH PERFECT RESULTS
Always cut potatoes into even sizes so that they cook evenly, and keep the water at a gentle simmer. If it boils furiously, the outsides of the potatoes will cook too quickly and become waterlogged.

BROCCOLI SLAW

SERVES 6

This is a lovely healthy side salad that provides just the crunch you need with the soft pork butt. Using yoghurt instead of oil in the dressing gives a hint of creaminess without the cloying richness you sometimes get with mayonnaise. Photograph overleaf.

1 head of broccoli
1 banana shallot (if unavailable, use 3 small ordinary shallots), peeled and finely diced
100g currants
100g whole blanched almonds, toasted and roughly chopped

FOR THE DRESSING
200ml natural yoghurt
1–1½ tbsp cider vinegar
Pinch of sugar
Sea salt and freshly ground black pepper

1. Cut off and discard the broccoli stalks, then chop the heads into small pieces. Place in a salad bowl and add the shallot, almonds and currants. Set aside.

2. Put the yoghurt for the dressing into a bowl and stir in the vinegar, starting with 1 tablespoon, and adding more later if needed. Add the sugar, mix well and season. Taste and add the remaining vinegar or a little extra sugar if necessary.

3. Pour the dressing over the broccoli, toss well and serve.

CRUSHED POTATOES WITH SPRING ONIONS AND CHEESE (RECIPE PAGE 233)

BROCCOLI SLAW (RECIPE PAGE 233)

SLOW-COOKED SMOKY PORK BUTT WITH CHIPOTLE MAYO (RECIPE PAGE 232)

STUFFED RIB OF BEEF

SERVES 6–8

The Sunday Roast is the cornerstone of home cooking and a rib of beef is the ultimate. Cooking beef on the bone not only looks impressive, but it gives the meat more flavour and ensures that it cooks evenly too. I'd be proud to serve this very simply, with juices from the pan, but as a twist, I'm stuffing it with mushrooms, spinach and tarragon and adding a mustard glaze. Delicious, especially when paired with Horseradish Yorkshire Puddings (page 239).

3-bone rib of beef on the bone, about 3.5–4.5kg, chine bone (spine) removed
2 heaped tsp English mustard powder
6 carrots, peeled and halved lengthways
6 parsnips, peeled and halved lengthways

FOR THE STUFFING
1 onion, peeled and finely diced
200g Portobello or chestnut mushrooms, wiped clean and finely chopped
3 garlic cloves, peeled and chopped
300g baby spinach
75g breadcrumbs made from stale bread (1 or 2 days old)
2 tarragon sprigs, leaves only, roughly chopped
1 lemon thyme sprig, leaves only
1 free-range egg yolk
Olive oil
Sea salt and freshly ground black pepper

CONTINUED FROM PAGE 237

1. Take the beef out of the fridge and allow it to come up to room temperature (about 1 hour). At that point, preheat the oven to 230°C/Gas 8.

2. Meanwhile, make the stuffing. Place a heavy-based sauté pan over a medium heat and add a dash of oil. When hot, add the onion with a pinch of salt and pepper and sauté until softened. Add the mushrooms and cook until tender. Add the garlic and sauté for 2 minutes, then add the spinach, in batches if necessary. Once the leaves have completely wilted, remove the pan from the heat and finely chop. Transfer to a bowl and allow to cool slightly.

3. Add the breadcrumbs and herbs to the stuffing, and stir well. Taste and adjust the seasoning as necessary. Stir in the egg yolk to bind the mixture.

4. Place the beef on a chopping board with the ribs on the right-hand side. Insert the tip of a sharp knife on the left-hand side of the meat about 3cm in from the edge and make a long incision just above the ribs, going two-thirds of the way into the joint. The idea is to separate the meat from the bones, but leave it attached along the bottom.

5. Gently pull the meat apart and push the stuffing into the gap. It might not take all the stuffing, in which case, put the excess in a small ovenproof dish, cover with a lid or foil, and bake it for the last 10–15 minutes of the meat cooking time.

6. Tie a couple of pieces of string horizontally around the meat and vertically between the rib bones to secure the stuffing in place. Put the mustard powder in a bowl with a pinch of salt and pepper and enough olive oil to form a thin paste. Rub the mixture into the meat.

7. Place the carrots and parsnips into the roasting tin. Drizzle with olive oil. Put the meat on top of the vegetables and roast for 15 minutes to brown the outside of the meat. Lower the temperature to 180°C/Gas 4 and continue roasting for 15 minutes per 450g of meat, plus 15 extra minutes at the end if you like rare beef (the internal temperature should register 50–53°C on a meat thermometer) or for a further 20–30 minutes if you prefer beef medium rare (internal temperature 54–57°C).

8. Remove the vegetables after 35 minutes and set aside ready to reheat before serving.

9. Once cooked, remove the beef from the oven, cover loosely with foil and leave to rest for at least 20 minutes, and anything up to 45 minutes.

10. To serve, place the vegetables back in the oven at 180°C for 15 minutes to finish cooking and reheat. Remove the string from the beef and slice away the rib bones, then carve the meat and spoon the stuffing and vegetables on to a serving platter.

HOW TO STORE RIB OF BEEF
Rib of beef should be kept unwrapped in the fridge so that it almost air dries. This will intensify the flavour and make it roast more quickly.

HORSERADISH YORKSHIRE PUDDINGS

MAKES 12

How can you improve on the traditional accompaniment to roast beef? you might ask. By adding the other roast beef essential – horseradish – of course. People often complain that their puddings don't rise properly. There are two secrets: get the oil or fat really hot before adding the batter, and once they are in the oven, no opening the oven door until they are all puffed up and majestic. Photograph on previous page.

150g plain flour
½ tsp salt
4 free-range eggs, beaten
200ml whole milk
6 tbsp freshly grated horseradish or 3 tbsp
    creamed horseradish
4 tbsp vegetable oil, duck fat or dripping

1. Preheat the oven to 230°C/Gas 8. If you are cooking these puddings to go with roast beef, increase the oven temperature once you remove the beef to rest.

2. Sift the flour and salt into a large bowl. Add the eggs and half the milk and beat until smooth. Mix in the remaining milk and the grated horseradish and leave the batter to rest for at least 30 minutes, or even while the beef cooks.

3. Put a teaspoon of oil or, better still, hot fat from the beef roasting tin into each compartment of a 12-hole muffin tin or 2 x 4 hole Yorkshire pudding tins and place on the top shelf of the oven until very hot (almost smoking).

4. When ready, whisk the batter again, pour it into a jug and fill the tin at the oven until each hole is three-quarters full. (This is safer than carrying a pan of boiling fat across the kitchen.) Watch out as the oil will sizzle a bit. Put the tin straight back into the oven and bake for 10–12 minutes for the 2 x 4 hole tins or 12–14 minutes for the muffin tin, until the Yorkshires are well risen, golden brown and crisp on the outside but soft and springy in the middle.

AROMATIC LAMB CHOPS WITH MINTY YOGHURT

SERVES 4

Spring lamb is one of the season's greatest gifts to a chef and should always be served very simply. But as the lamb matures through the year and the meat develops more flavour, you can afford to get more adventurous. This simple spice mix of cumin, coriander, turmeric and ginger isn't too overpowering but really enhances lamb's natural sweetness. A cooling spoonful of minted yoghurt and a simple salad, like my Chargrilled Broccoli and Bulgur Salad (page 241) are all the sides it needs.

2 tsp cumin seeds
2 tsp coriander seeds
1 tsp ground turmeric
4cm piece of fresh root ginger, peeled and
    finely grated
2 garlic cloves, peeled and finely grated
Olive oil, for marinade
8–12 lamb cutlets, French trimmed
250ml natural yoghurt
4 mint sprigs, leaves only, roughly chopped
Sea salt and freshly ground black pepper

1. Put the seeds and turmeric into a mortar, add a pinch of salt and pound as finely as possible. Mix in the ginger and garlic, then add a little olive oil to form a paste.

2. Rub the paste into the lamb and leave to marinate for a while (anywhere from 10 minutes to overnight).

3. Place a griddle pan over a medium heat and drizzle with oil. When hot, add the lamb and griddle it for 3–4 minutes on either side if you like it pink, or 4–6 minutes if you prefer it well done. When cooked to your liking, turn the lamb on edge and cook the fat until dark golden and crisp.

4. Put the yoghurt and mint into a bowl, season with salt and pepper and mix well.

5. Serve the cutlets with the yoghurt on the side.

CHARGRILLED BROCCOLI AND BULGUR SALAD
SERVES 4

This North African salad is great warm or cold. Serve it with the Aromatic Lamb Cutlets with Minty Yoghurt (page 240) – the flavours really complement one another.

150g bulgur
300g broccoli, separated into medium florets
Sea salt and freshly ground black pepper

FOR THE DRESSING
Bunch of mint, leaves only
1–2 tsp harissa paste, or to taste
150ml buttermilk

1. Cook the bulgur according to the packet instructions. Transfer to a serving bowl.

2. Place a large heavy-based frying pan over a medium heat. Add the broccoli to the dry pan, season with a pinch of salt and cook for 6–10 minutes, until the broccoli is charred in places and tender. Add to the bulgur.

3. To make the dressing, finely chop half the mint leaves. Place them in a bowl with 1 teaspoon of the harissa, the buttermilk and a pinch of salt and pepper and mix well. Taste and adjust the seasoning, adding more harissa if you want a spicier flavour.

4. Pour the dressing over the bulgur and broccoli, add the whole mint leaves and toss well before serving.

USING BUTTERMILK
Buttermilk is the thin, slightly sour liquid left after churning butter. It is often used in dressings, baking and to tenderise meat. It is widely available but if you can't find any, substitute it with two parts plain yoghurt and one part milk.

PUDDINGS

A LOT OF PEOPLE WHEN COOKING FOR FRIENDS WILL MANAGE A STARTER AND MAIN COURSE, BUT RUN OUT OF STEAM WHEN IT GETS TO PUDDING.

There's no great shame in that – after all, in France they invariably buy in dessert from a patisserie and it's never seen as a failure on the host's part – but I guarantee that if you do go to the extra effort of making dessert, your guests will love you for it. In a way, dessert is the most social of all the courses – when you go out for dinner it's the one course where friends will tend to taste a bit of everyone else's. It creates a buzz, a grand finale, and it's the memory guests will go away with. The same applies at home, so personally I always like to end the night on a sweet note. It needn't be anything hugely complicated and it certainly needn't be time-consuming to make but it just leaves everyone in a good mood, with a feeling that they have been well looked after.

Of all the courses, this is the one to have made in advance so when it comes to it, it's just a question of taking it out of the fridge or freezer, or putting it in the oven. You'll have been doing enough work between courses already, so do yourself a favour and make this last course as straightforward as possible. Trust me, this isn't the time to try your hand at making a soufflé for the first time. You'll find lots of suggestions in this chapter. Jellies are always brilliant because, well, we're all kids at heart and who doesn't like jelly? Especially a grown-up version with a little kick of alcohol. The same goes for ice creams, sorbets and mousses. They all have to be made in advance and will sit happily in the fridge or freezer until the moment you want to serve them. It's always a good idea to have tried-and-tested dishes like these ready and waiting. That way even if one of the other courses doesn't go according to plan (and believe me, that can happen to all of us), you'll panic less knowing that at least the finale will be a triumph.

I think the secret of a really successful pudding is to give it a twist. Make it adventurous and unexpected and your guests will be sure to remember it long after they go home. There are so many ways you can play with traditional desserts: add a little chilli and star anise to poached pears, some lavender to a traditional crème caramel, black pepper to a banana tarte tatin.

Actually, adding spice in general is a great way of jazzing up a familiar pudding. Even a simple bowl of strawberries can be livened up with a drizzle of balsamic vinegar and a twist of black pepper. Basil leaves do something similar to a lemon sorbet or granita. And my vanilla salt is a brilliant addition to thinly sliced pineapple. Both green cardamom and the more exotically perfumed black cardamom go perfectly with caramel-based puddings such as tarte tatin and also with chocolate. The slightly medicinal flavour of bay leaves works surprisingly well in sweet custards, especially when poured over an apple crumble. Or try adding rosemary and thyme in moderation to orange or raspberry jellies and the like.

When it comes to speed and simplicity, you won't go far wrong if you keep some ready-rolled puff or sweet shortcrust pastry to hand. Simply brush the pastry with a little warm jam, lay on slices of fruit – apple, pear or plum all work well – dust with icing sugar and bake in the oven until the pastry is cooked. My Pear and Ginger Galette recipe on page 267

is barely more complicated than that and makes a stunning pudding. Alternatively, the holy trinity of quick pudding ingredients are double cream (different creams have different uses according to their fat content so see my guide below), Greek yoghurt and frozen berries. If you have these three in your fridge or freezer you are only minutes away from a lovely fruit fool. Simply whisk the cream, add a little yoghurt to cut the richness and fold in icing sugar and berries to taste. Serve with a shortbread biscuit and you've got a pudding worthy of any dinner party. If you've got some meringues to crumble in, even better. You see, home cooking should never be over-elaborate and as I've said before, better a relaxed host and simple food than a stressed host and complex food.

CLOTTED CREAM

This is made by heating and cooling double cream, then skimming off the rich "clotted" crust. At 55 per cent butterfat, it's too thick to cook with but makes a luxurious accompaniment to scones or puddings.

DOUBLE CREAM

At nearly 50 per cent butterfat, double cream is a versatile, general purpose cream ideal for desserts and ice-cream. Once whipped it can be very dense, so I sometimes mix it with Greek yoghurt to make it less heavy.

WHIPPING CREAM

At 35 per cent butterfat, this is thinner and slightly healthier than double cream but, as the name suggests, still holds its shape well when whipped. As with double cream you have to be careful not to overbeat it, or it will become granular. If this happens, add a splash more cream and beat it slowly until smooth again.

SINGLE CREAM

About 20 per cent butterfat, single cream is ideal for pouring over puddings or for enriching soups and sauces. It is not suitable for boiling as it will curdle.

CRÈME FRAÎCHE

A mix of sour and fresh cream, crème fraîche has a lovely tangy flavour. It will never curdle or separate when boiled and, because it is naturally thick, is ideal for garnishing soups.

CHOCOLATE

As with wine and coffee, there has been an explosion of interest in the provenance of proper chocolate recently. More and more people are starting to understand how different 70 per cent Valrhona, say, is from a bar of Bournville. From the home cook's point of view, this is fantastic because it means it's no longer just the professional chefs who have access to chocolate with higher levels of cocoa solids. Believe me, when cooking with chocolate, it really is a case of getting out what you put in. Even when making something for the children, I'll always use high-quality. You can always add more sugar or cream to make it more appealing to young taste buds.

PINEAPPLE CARPACCIO WITH
POMEGRANATE AND VANILLA SALT

APEROL SPRITZ JELLY

LEMON AND BASIL GRANITA

BANANA AND COCONUT FRITTERS

SPICED BANANA TARTE TATIN

LAVENDAR CRÈME CARAMEL

ESPRESSO PANNA COTTA WITH
CINNAMON HAZELNUT BRITTLE

ETON MESS BOMBE

PEAR AND GINGER GALETTE

MANGO PARFAIT POTS WITH
MACERATED BERRIES

WHITE CHOCOLATE AND LIME MOUSSE

APPLE COMPOTE WITH
A CREAMY WHIP

STEAMED DATE PUDDING WITH
BUTTERSCOTCH SAUCE

HAZELNUT MERINGUE TOWER

CHILLI POACHED PEARS WITH
STAR ANISE DUST

CHOCOLATE AND PISTACHIO
SEMIFREDDO

PINEAPPLE CARPACCIO WITH POMEGRANATE AND VANILLA SALT

SERVES 4

This is a light, healthy pudding to intrigue your guests with. It may sound strange but the combination of salt, vanilla and very thinly sliced pineapple really works well.

1 large ripe pineapple
1 pomegranate
Small bunch of mint, leaves shredded

FOR THE VANILLA SALT
125g sea salt or fleur de sel
1 vanilla pod, split open and seeds scraped out

1. First make the vanilla salt. Put the salt and vanilla seeds into a bowl and mix well. Place in an airtight container with the empty pod and use as required in baking or savoury dishes. The mixture will keep indefinitely.

2. Cut off the ends of the pineapple, then slice off the skin from top to bottom, keeping the fruit whole. Cut the pineapple widthways into slices about 1mm thick so you end up with lots of circles. Set aside.

3. Cut the pomegranate in half horizontally. Hold each half in turn over a bowl and smack the skin with the back of a wooden spoon so that the seeds drop into the bowl. Reserve any juice that comes out of the seeds as you remove them.

4. To serve, sprinkle a serving platter with a little vanilla salt. Arrange the pineapple slices over it, then sprinkle with a little extra vanilla salt, the pomegranate seeds and juice. Finish with a light sprinkling of the vanilla salt and the shredded mint leaves.

USING SALT IN SWEET DISHES
Adding a little salt to sweet dishes actually enhances the sweetness. I often add a pinch to cakes, biscuits and especially caramel sauces. Vanilla salt would work well in all of these, too. Try it also sprinkled over a buttery fillet of white fish.

APEROL SPRITZ JELLY

SERVES 4

Aperol is a bitter-sweet Italian aperitif made from herbs and roots, a little like Campari. If you go into a bar in northern Italy, especially Venice, you'll see people drinking Spritz, a refreshing drink made of Aperol, prosecco and sparkling water and often garnished with a slice of orange. I think you can see where I got the idea for this jelly from.

7 sheets of leaf gelatine
1 x 750ml bottle prosecco
150g caster sugar
6 tbsp Aperol
4 thin slices of orange

1. Place the gelatine sheets in a small bowl of cold water and leave for 5–10 minutes, until softened.

2. Pour 100ml water and a quarter of the prosecco into a saucepan, add the sugar and warm over a low heat, stirring occasionally, until the sugar has dissolved.

3. Squeeze out the gelatine and add to the saucepan, off the heat, stirring until dissolved. Strain the mixture into a jug and set aside until cool.

4. Add the Aperol and remaining prosecco to the jug and stir well.

5. Take 4 tumblers (about 250ml capacity) and insert an orange slice in each one, positioning it diagonally. Carefully pour in the Aperol mixture, sharing it equally between the glasses. Chill overnight or until set (at least 4 hours).

USING FRUIT IN JELLIES
Individual jellies using fruit such as strawberries or raspberries need to be set in two stages – otherwise the fruit will float to the top. Using single orange or lemon slices makes the whole process easier because they can be wedged against the sides of the glass.

LEMON AND BASIL GRANITA

SERVES 4

This is a lovely refreshing ice that we sometimes serve as a palate-cleansing pre-dessert in the restaurants. The pepperiness of the basil and freshness of the lemon work really well together. Granitas are great things to make at home because you don't need an ice cream maker or have to worry about getting a smooth texture – the whole point of them is that they are granular. They are best made and eaten on the same day, though, or they can become blocks of ice.

7 unwaxed lemons – zest from 1 and juice from all
150ml water
150g caster sugar
4 basil sprigs, leaves only

1. Put the lemon zest into a small saucepan, strain in the juice and add the sugar. Stir over a medium heat until the sugar has dissolved. Allow to cool for 5 minutes.

2. Dilute the mixture with the water to taste. Set aside 4 small basil leaves for decoration, then very finely chop the rest. Add to the lemon mixture.

3. Pour the syrup into a lidded plastic container and freeze for 3 hours, or until frozen at the bottom and around the edges. Swirl the mixture with a fork to break up the ice crystals, then cover and return to the freezer for another hour. Repeat this freezing and stirring process twice more before letting the granita freeze solid with a granular texture.

4. To serve, break up the granita with the fork, then spoon into chilled serving glasses. Garnish with the reserved basil leaves and serve immediately.

BANANA AND COCONUT FRITTERS

MAKES 12–16

This is a dish I discovered when I was travelling around Asia and it has since become a firm favourite. Asian food – certainly that of Thailand and Vietnam – uses almost no dairy products so this is basically their take on a milk- and egg-free pancake. It's also a great way to use up any bananas that are turning black in the fruit bowl. As far as these fritters are concerned, the riper they are, the better!

125g plain flour
1 tsp baking powder
75g caster sugar, plus extra for sprinkling
25g desiccated coconut
Finely grated zest of 1 lime
Pinch of salt
4 ripe bananas, peeled and mashed (about 400g flesh in total)
Vegetable oil, for frying

1. Sift the flour and baking powder into a large bowl. Stir in the sugar, coconut, lime zest and salt. Stir the mashed bananas into the dry ingredients, mixing until well combined. Cover the batter with cling film and chill for 15 minutes.

2. Fill a large saucepan one-third full of oil and heat to 180°C, or until a cube of bread dropped in the oil sizzles and turns golden in 30 seconds.

3. Using a tablespoon, carefully drop 4 or 5 spoonfuls of the batter into the hot oil and fry for 2–3 minutes, until golden brown on both sides and cooked through.

4. Lift out with a slotted spoon, drain on kitchen paper, and repeat with the rest of the mixture. Serve hot, sprinkled with a little sugar.

SPICED BANANA TARTE TATIN

SERVES 6

This twist on the famous French apple or pear tarte tatin is not only one of the easiest desserts in the world to make but one of the most delicious. It also shows just how brilliantly unusual combinations can work. Black pepper provides the heat and the pink peppercorns a mild fruitiness. I never bother making my own puff pastry at home – just make sure you buy an all-butter one.

50g butter, softened
1 vanilla pod, split open and seeds scraped out
½ tsp pink peppercorns, crushed in a mortar
½ tsp black peppercorns, crushed in a mortar
100g caster sugar
6 large ripe bananas, peeled
320g ready-rolled sheet of all-butter puff pastry

1. Preheat the oven to 200°C/Gas 6.

2. Spread the butter evenly across the base of a 20cm ovenproof frying pan. Add both the vanilla pod and seeds. Top with a third of the crushed peppercorns, then sprinkle over the sugar.

3. Peel the bananas and cut into pieces 3–4cm thick. Arrange them, cut side down, in concentric circles in the pan so that they are the same height as the rim. Sprinkle over another third of the crushed peppercorns.

4. Unroll the pastry sheet and, using a plate slightly larger than the top of the pan, cut out a circle. Drape the pastry over the bananas and tuck the edges down the sides of the pan with the back of a spoon. Pierce the pastry a few times with the tip of a sharp knife.

5. Place the pan over a medium–high heat for 3–4 minutes, until the sugar dissolves, then shake gently as it caramelises to a toffee colour and starts to bubble up the sides. Transfer to the oven and bake for 30–35 minutes, until the pastry is golden brown. Leave the tarte to stand for 10 minutes, then invert it carefully onto a serving dish.

6. Remove the vanilla pod, sprinkle the tarte with the remaining crushed peppercorns, then cut into wedges and serve.

HOW TO MAKE THE PERFECT TARTE TATIN
It's important to make a couple of holes in the pastry lid, otherwise the steam caught underneath will stop the pastry from cooking. Before turning out the tarte, give it a quick blast of heat on the hob, shaking the pan slightly to help to release the fruit cleanly from the caramel.

LAVENDER CRÈME CARAMEL
SERVES 4

A properly made crème caramel, rich with vanilla seeds and dripping with caramel, is an all-time classic. I've mainly stuck with tradition here, but the hint of lavender gives it another dimension. You can buy lavender sugar and edible flowers from some supermarkets, but it's easy to make your own. Simply put dried unsprayed (i.e. edible) lavender sprigs into golden caster sugar and store in an airtight container. The longer the lavender is left in the sugar, the more intense the flavour. I also like to use lavender sugar when making shortbread.

150g golden caster sugar
1 tsp lavender flowers, plus a few extra
    for decoration
Butter, for greasing
500ml whole milk
4 free-range eggs
Seeds from 1 vanilla pod
50g lavender sugar

1. Preheat the oven to 150°C/Gas 2. Set out 4 x 150ml ramekins.

2. Put the first quantity of sugar into a small, heavy-based pan over a medium-low heat and allow it to dissolve completely. At that point, turn up the heat and boil briefly until it becomes a dark golden caramel (2–3 minutes).

3. Pour the caramel into the ramekins straight away, dividing it equally, and sprinkle each one with a couple of lavender flowers. Set aside to cool (not in the fridge). Once the caramel has set, grease the insides of the ramekins with a thin layer of butter.

4. Place the milk in a saucepan and warm gently over a low heat until just below scalding point.

5. Meanwhile, put the eggs, vanilla seeds and lavender sugar into a bowl and whisk thoroughly. Gradually pour the hot milk into the egg mixture, whisking as you do so, until completely smooth. Transfer the mixture to a jug for the next step.

6. Place the ramekins in a lined roasting tin (see tip below) and fill them with the custard, dividing it equally between them. Pour boiling water into the tray until it comes halfway up the sides of the dishes (being careful not to get any splashes in the custard).

7. Carefully transfer the bain-marie to the oven and cook the puddings for 25–35 minutes, until set but with a slight wobble in the middle.

8. Remove the dishes from the tin and allow to cool. This is best done overnight in the fridge so that the caramel and custard can properly combine.

9. To serve, loosen the crème caramels by dipping the ramekins in hot water and running a knife around the inside edge. Place a plate over each ramekin and, holding tightly, invert both, giving the dish a little shake if necessary. Serve decorated with the remaining lavender flowers.

HOW TO MAKE PERFECT CUSTARD
When making custard, it is important to take the milk off the heat just before it boils. Also, only whisk together the sugar and eggs at the last minute, otherwise the yolks will start to become runny.

ESPRESSO PANNA COTTA WITH CINNAMON HAZELNUT BRITTLE

SERVES 4

Panna cotta, or 'cooked cream', is the posh Italian equivalent of our own blancmange and all the more delicious. It's very easy to make and can be flavoured with anything you like, from vanilla or lemon to rose or chocolate. My coffee-flavoured version is distinctly grown-up, especially when served with a nut brittle. I've used hazelnuts here, but almonds, walnuts or pecans would all work just as well.

3 sheets of leaf gelatine
400ml double cream
75ml whole milk
100g caster sugar
50ml espresso shot (if unavailable, replace with
    1½ tbsp coffee granules dissolved in 50ml
    boiling water)

FOR THE BRITTLE
50g blanched hazelnuts
200g caster sugar
1 tsp ground cinnamon

1. Place the gelatine sheets in a small bowl of cold water and leave for 5–10 minutes, until softened. Set out 4 x 175ml dariole moulds or ramekins.

2. Put the cream, milk, sugar and coffee into a small heavy-based saucepan. Place over a medium-low heat and bring to a simmer. Immediately remove from the heat.

3. Squeeze out the soaked gelatine leaves and stir them into the hot cream, mixing well until completely dissolved. Set aside to cool slightly.

4. Meanwhile, rinse the moulds or ramekins in cold water, but don't dry them. This will make the panna cottas easier to turn out once set. Pour the panna cotta mixture through a sieve into a jug, then pour into the waiting moulds. Place in the fridge and leave to set overnight.

5. Preheat the oven to 180°C/Gas 4.

6. Meanwhile, make the brittle. Put the hazelnuts on a baking tray and place in the oven for 10 minutes, or until golden.

7. Line another baking tray with greaseproof paper or a silicon mat. Sprinkle the sugar into a heavy-based frying pan and place over a medium heat until the sugar dissolves and begins to turn golden. Swirl the pan to ensure it caramelises evenly. Once it is dark golden, add the toasted hazelnuts and ground cinnamon, swirl to combine, then tip into the prepared baking tray. Set aside until completely hard.

8. To serve, dip the moulds in boiling water for 5 seconds. Place a plate over each one and, holding tightly, invert both, giving the mould a little shake if necessary. Break the brittle into shards and serve alongside the panna cottas.

HOW TO COOL CARAMEL
Never put caramel in the refrigerator to cool as it will go sticky and soggy. Room temperature is best.

ETON MESS BOMBE

SERVES 8–10

Everyone loves Eton mess, but as the name suggests, it's not the most elegant-looking dessert. So my twist is to freeze it in a pudding basin and then turn it out before serving. Pour over a strawberry coulis and top with grated chocolate and its makeover from nursery food to dinner party show-stopper is complete.

800g strawberries, hulled
Icing sugar, for dusting
800ml double cream
4–6 best-quality individual meringues or
   1 large meringue
50g white or dark chocolate to serve (you could
   also use dark chocolate flavoured with mint)

1. Cut the strawberries into quarters. Dust half of them in icing sugar and place in a small pan over a medium heat for 3–4 minutes, until the fruit begins to break down.

2. Blitz the hot strawberries in a blender, then push them through a sieve placed over a bowl to remove the seeds and create a smooth coulis. Set aside to cool.

3. Meanwhile, whip the cream until it begins to thicken, but before it reaches soft peak. Break the meringue(s) into bite-sized pieces, add to the cream and gently fold in.

4. Lightly stir half the coulis and all the reserved strawberries into the cream to create a ripple effect (this will look good when serving). Transfer the mixture to a 2 litre pudding basin lightly oiled and lined with 3 layers of cling film, cover with more cling film and freeze overnight, or for at least 2½ hours.

5. To serve, carefully run hot tap water around the outside of the frozen basin until the pudding can be released. Remove the cling film and invert the pudding onto a serving plate. Drizzle with the remaining coulis, finely grate the chocolate over it and serve.

HOW TO WHIP CREAM
Always whip cream by hand because you'll get more of a feel for the texture, especially when you want a looser, three-quarter whip. Do it in bursts – 10 seconds on, 10 seconds off – to give your arm a chance to recover.

PEAR AND GINGER GALETTE

SERVES 4

This shows just how quick and easy it can be to make a fruit tart, especially if you take the cheat's option of ready-made pastry (in which case you'll need a 320g sheet of all-butter sweet shortcrust). You don't even need a tart tin because the crimped edges keep everything in place. I like to make one large tart for a family supper, but you could make individual ones for a more formal dinner.

4 pears, peeled, quartered and cored
1 tbsp demerara sugar
1 ball of preserved stem ginger, finely chopped
2 tbsp stem ginger syrup
3cm piece of fresh root ginger, peeled and finely grated
Zest of 1 lemon
1 free-range egg yolk
Icing sugar, for dusting
Cream, to serve

FOR THE SWEET SHORTCRUST PASTRY
225g plain flour
2 tbsp icing sugar
150g cold butter, diced
Zest of 1 lemon
1 free-range egg, beaten

1. Preheat the oven to 180°C/Gas 4. Line a baking sheet with greaseproof or baking paper.

2. First make the pastry. Sift the flour and icing sugar into a bowl. Add the butter and rub it in with your fingertips until the mixture resembles coarse breadcrumbs. Stir in the lemon zest, then add the egg and mix to combine. Gradually add just enough ice-cold water (1–2 tablespoons) to form a dough. Knead lightly into a smooth ball, then wrap in cling film and chill for at least 30 minutes.

3. When ready, flour a work surface and roll out the pastry to a thickness of 4mm (slightly thicker than a £1 coin). Place a 22cm dinner plate upside-down on the pastry and cut around it. Transfer the pastry circle to the prepared baking sheet. The excess pastry can be set aside for use in another dish or frozen.

4. Mix together the pears, demerara sugar, both gingers, the ginger syrup and half the lemon zest.

5. Arrange the pears in a neat pattern around the centre of the pastry, leaving a 3cm empty border around the edge. Brush the border with the beaten egg yolk.

6. Fold up the pastry border around the pears, crimping it into a wavy 'wall'. Brush the top of the pastry rim with more egg wash, then dust everything with icing sugar. Sprinkle the remaining lemon zest over the top and bake for 30–35 minutes, until the pastry is golden and the pears tender and caramelising slightly.

7. Dust the finished tart with a light sprinkling of icing sugar, then slice and serve with a little pouring cream.

MANGO PARFAIT POTS WITH MACERATED BERRIES
SERVES 4

A parfait is normally made with eggs and whipped cream, but using yoghurt sweetened only with fruit, as here, makes it less rich but no less luxurious. Do look out for Indian Alphonso mangoes during their short season in May and June. Their sweet perfumed flesh is unrivalled. If this all sounds too healthy, you could always add a bit of alcohol to the macerated berries. Cointreau or Crème de cassis would both be good.

1 ripe mango
500ml natural yoghurt

FOR THE MACERATED FRUIT
200g mixed berries, e.g. blackberries, raspberries and strawberries, hulled and quartered or halved
Zest and juice of 1 small orange
1 tbsp icing sugar
Small handful of basil leaves, finely shredded

1. First prepare the berries. Place them in a bowl and add the orange zest, sugar and basil. Mix well, cover with cling film and set aside to macerate for an hour or two.

2. Meanwhile, peel the mango and remove the stone. Purée the flesh in a blender until smooth. Layer the purée and yoghurt in 4 x 200ml serving glasses and chill until required. (If you have time, you might like to alternate the layers to create a stripy effect.)

3. When ready to serve, top each glass with the macerated berries.

HOW TO FREEZE PARFAITS
Parfaits can easily be made in advance, if preferred, and then frozen. Remove them from the freezer 10 minutes before serving to allow them to temper.

WHITE CHOCOLATE AND LIME MOUSSE

SERVES 4

Here's a stunningly simple crowd-pleasing dessert that brings together the classic flavours of chocolate, cream, raspberries and mint. The lime zest not only looks pretty but helps cut the richness of the mousse.

100g white chocolate
300ml double cream
Zest of 1 lime, plus extra to garnish
3 large free-range eggs, whites only
50g caster sugar
150g raspberries
3 mint sprigs, leaves torn or finely shredded

1. Break the chocolate into small pieces and place in a heatproof bowl.

2. Place half the cream in a small saucepan and heat until it begins to boil. Pour it immediately over the chocolate and stir until the mixture is smooth. Place the lime zest and the rest of the cream into another bowl and whisk until it forms soft peaks. Fold this mixture into the melted chocolate. Set aside.

3. In a separate bowl, whisk the egg whites until they form soft peaks. Whisk in the sugar a tablespoon at a time, and continue whisking until the mixture is shiny, smooth and has stiff peaks that hold their shape. Carefully fold it into the chocolate mixture.

4. Set some raspberries aside for garnish, place the rest together with the mint into 4 x 200ml glasses or a 1 litre serving bowl. Crush the fruit lightly with a fork. Spoon the chocolate mousse over the raspberries, garnish with a few extra fresh raspberries and sprinkle with grated white chocolate and lime zest and chill for at least 2 hours, or overnight if you have the time.

THE SECRET TO PERFECTLY WHISKED EGG WHITES
To whisk egg whites you need a spotlessly clean bowl and beaters. Any grease will stop the whites from forming peaks.

APPLE COMPOTE WITH A CREAMY WHIP

SERVES 6

At heart this is just stewed apples and cream, but it shows how, if you want to, you can enhance every component of a dish to create something greater than the sum of its parts. I love the taste of caramelised apples in a tarte tatin, so why not recreate the same effect here, with some spices thrown in for good measure? And by adding beaten egg whites to the cream, you end up with a topping as light as snow.

250g caster sugar
2 dessert apples e.g. Braeburn, peeled, cored and chopped into chunks
2 Bramley apples, peeled, cored and chopped into chunks
3cm piece of fresh root ginger, peeled and thickly sliced

3 small cinnamon sticks
75g butter
2 free-range egg whites
250ml double cream
Zest of 1 lemon

1. Sprinkle 200g of the sugar into a hot heavy-based pan in an even layer. Heat without stirring until it becomes a golden caramel, swirling the pan now and again for an even colour.

2. Add the apples, ginger and cinnamon sticks and swirl so that everything is coated in the caramel. Cook over a low heat for 5 minutes, then add the butter. Cook for a further 5 minutes, or until the apples are soft and collapsing.

3. Pour the mixture into a sieve set over a bowl and allow to drain. Reserve the liquid.

4. Remove the ginger and cinnamon from the apple mixture, then spoon the fruit into 6 x 175ml serving glasses. Reserve any excess cooking juices. Chill for an hour or so.

5. Meanwhile, whisk the egg whites until they form soft peaks. Now whisk in the remaining sugar a little at a time, until the mixture forms stiff, glossy peaks.

6. In a separate bowl, whip the cream until thickened and just reaching soft peaks. Add three-quarters of the lemon zest and gently mix, then stir in the remaining apple liquid (you can reserve some to drizzle on top, if liked). Finally, fold the egg whites into the cream mixture until combined.

7. Spoon or pipe the cream mixture over each chilled dish of apple compote. Sprinkle over the remaining lemon zest and, if you like, drizzle over any reserved cooking juices. Chill for 30 minutes before serving.

STEAMED DATE PUDDING WITH BUTTERSCOTCH SAUCE

SERVES 6–8

There are some dishes you shouldn't mess with, and this is one of them. Just thinking about it makes me feel like a kid again. In an age of microwaves and fast food, it may seem odd having to steam a pudding for two hours, but this old-fashioned dessert well rewards the time you invest, I promise.

200g self-raising flour
75g suet
75g walnut halves, chopped
175g pitted Medjool dates, roughly chopped
Finely grated zest of 1 orange
3 tbsp light muscovado sugar, or light brown sugar
1 heaped tbsp black treacle
1 free-range egg
200ml whole milk

FOR THE BUTTERSCOTCH SAUCE
100g butter
75g soft light brown sugar
75g golden syrup
Pinch of coarse sea salt
Seeds from 1 vanilla pod
300ml double cream

1. Grease an 850ml pudding basin and line the bottom with a circle of baking paper. Cut another circle of baking paper about 5cm bigger than the top of the basin and make a 2cm pleat in the middle.

2. Sift the flour into a large bowl, then add the suet, walnuts, dates, orange zest, sugar and treacle and stir together.

3. In a separate bowl, lightly beat the egg, then add the milk and mix well. Slowly pour this liquid into the flour mixture, stirring constantly until well incorporated. Pour into the prepared pudding basin. Place the pleated paper circle on top of the pudding and cover with pleated foil. Tie securely in place with string, looping it across the top to make a handle.

4. Put a trivet or heatproof saucer in a large saucepan. Sit the pudding on top and pour in enough water to come halfway up the sides of the basin. Cover the pan with a tight-fitting lid, bring to the boil, then simmer gently for 2–2¼ hours, topping up the water as necessary. When cooked, lift the pudding out of the water and leave it to sit for 5 minutes.

5. Meanwhile, make the sauce. Put the butter, sugar, syrup, salt and vanilla seeds into a small saucepan and place over a medium heat until everything has melted together. Stir in the cream and bubble for 5 minutes, until the mixture has thickened slightly.

6. Unwrap the pudding, invert it onto a serving plate and remove the small paper circle. Serve wedges or spoonfuls of the pudding with a generous drizzle of the butterscotch sauce.

USING SUET
Suet has fallen out of favour but is a feature of many classic British puddings, from Jam Roly-poly to Spotted Dick. It adds texture and depth of flavour to your cooking, but if you prefer, you can grate in frozen butter as an alternative.

HAZELNUT MERINGUE TOWER

SERVES 6–8

Guests are always impressed by home-made meringues, especially when presented with a towering chocolate cream sandwich like this. There are all sorts of theories about how to make the best meringues – using icing sugar instead of caster, adding a teaspoon of vinegar to the egg whites – but the most important thing is to bake them very slowly in a low oven. You're not really cooking them as such, just drying them out.

4 free-range egg whites, at room temperature
225g golden caster sugar
25g ground hazelnuts
25g chopped hazelnuts

FOR THE FILLING
300g dark chocolate (70 per cent cocoa solids), broken into pieces
400ml double cream

1. Preheat the oven to 140°C/Gas 1. Line three baking sheets with greaseproof or baking paper.

2. Whisk the egg whites in a large, scrupulously clean bowl until they form stiff peaks. Whisk in the sugar a spoonful at a time until the mixture is glossy and holding its shape. Finally, fold in the ground and chopped hazelnuts.

3. Put a dab of the meringue mixture under each corner of the paper on the prepared sheets to keep it in place. Now spoon equal amounts of the mixture into the middle of each sheet and shape each mound into a circle about 18cm wide.

4. Bake in the oven for 1½ hours, or until crisp on the outside and still a little soft in the middle. Turn off the oven and let the meringues cool inside with the door slightly ajar. When completely cold, they can be stored in an airtight container for a week.

5. When you're ready to serve, make the filling. Place the chocolate in a heatproof bowl over a pan of simmering water (it must not actually touch the water) and warm until melted. Set aside to cool for 5 minutes.

6. In a separate bowl, whisk the cream until it forms soft peaks. Mix three-quarters of the melted chocolate into the cream and fold in quickly and thoroughly, being careful not to overwork it.

7. Choose the best meringue for the top, then place one of the other meringues on a cake stand or serving plate. Spread half the chocolate cream over it with a spatula. Place the second meringue on top and cover with the remaining cream mixture. Sit the final meringue on the stack and drizzle the remaining melted chocolate over it.

HOW TO SPREAD MERINGUE NESTS EVENLY
Put four blobs of meringue on the corners of a baking tray to anchor the greaseproof paper in place. It then makes it much easier to spread out the meringue in uniform nests.

CHILLI POACHED PEARS WITH STAR ANISE DUST

SERVES 4

This is one of those puddings that tastes so much more complex than it is, with the warming spices adding layers of interest to the sweet pears. I love cooking with star anise, which is one of the main ingredients in Chinese five-spice. I'll often add the star-shaped pods to stocks and syrups, as I do here, but grinding it to a powder and sprinkling it over the pears at the last moment also makes the dish beautifully fragrant.

125g caster sugar
1 red chilli, halved lengthways
Pinch of saffron (optional)
2 whole star anise
4 Conference pears, peeled

FOR THE DUST
4 star anise
1 tsp ground ginger

1. Trim a small slice off the bottom of the pears so that they sit upright when you come to serve them.

2. Put the sugar, chilli, saffron (if using) and the star anise into a saucepan large enough to hold the pears and add 500ml water. Place over a medium heat until the sugar has dissolved, then add the pears. Simmer gently for 8–10 minutes, until the pears are tender but still holding their shape.

3. Meanwhile, make the dust. Put the star anise into a mortar and grind to a powder using the pestle. Mix with the ground ginger, then store in a screwtop jar until needed.

4. When the pears are ready, remove them from the pan. Place the poaching liquor over a medium heat and reduce for 10-15 minutes until thickened and syrupy. Either serve immediately or set aside and allow the pears to cool in the syrup overnight – this will intensify the flavours.

5. Serve the pears warm or cold with a little syrup spooned over and some star anise dust sprinkled on top.

HOW TO CHOOSE PEARS FOR POACHING
The pears should be ripe but not soft or else they will lose their shape when you poach them. Try to leave the stalk on when you peel them for a more professional look.

CHOCOLATE AND PISTACHIO SEMIFREDDO

SERVES 10

The semifreddo (Italian for 'half-cold') is a bit like a cheat's ice cream. You don't have to make a custard base or churn it smooth in an ice cream maker, you simply combine beaten eggs, whipped cream and your flavouring and freeze it. In my book, that makes it the perfect make-ahead dinner party pudding.

Oil or butter, for greasing
275g dark chocolate (70 per cent cocoa solids), plus extra for decorating
4 free-range eggs
100g caster sugar
500ml double cream
Seeds from 1 vanilla pod
100g pistachio nuts, loose skin rubbed off

1. Lightly grease the inside of a 1kg loaf tin with oil or butter, then line it with two layers of cling film, leaving a generous overhang.

2. Break the chocolate into pieces and place in a heatproof bowl set over a pan of simmering water (it must not actually touch the water). Heat until melted, then stir well and set aside to cool for 5 minutes.

3. Meanwhile, place the eggs and sugar in another bowl and whisk for 3–4 minutes, until pale, thick and fluffy. When the whisk is raised the mixture should leave a trail on the surface.

4. Stir the cooled chocolate into the egg mixture.

5. Put the cream and vanilla seeds in a separate bowl and whisk until the mixture forms soft peaks.

6. Add the whipped cream to the chocolate mixture, then fold in the pistachios. Pour into the prepared loaf tin, cover with the overhanging cling film and freeze overnight, or for at least 3–4 hours. (In fact, it can be frozen for up to 2 weeks before you want to use it.)

7. Remove the semifreddo from the freezer 10 minutes before serving in order to soften a little. Run a table knife around the inside edges of the tin, then peel back the top cling film and turn the semifreddo onto a board or serving plate. Remove the rest of the cling film, then grate a little extra dark chocolate over the top before slicing and serving.

INDEX

**PAGE NUMBERS IN *ITALICS*
REFER TO PHOTOGRAPHS**

ACKNOWLEDGEMENTS

Firstly a massive thank you to my incredible wife Tana for her input and support and to our four children, Megan, Jack, Holly and Tilly for their involvement and for being such amazing sports. I could never do it without you.

The vision and commitment from the talented Hodder team – Nicky Ross, Sarah Hammond, Alasdair Oliver, Kate Brunt, Susan Spratt, Joanna Seaton and Eleni Lawrence – has made another exciting and engaging book possible.

I must mention the accomplished Tony Turnbull for his dedicated assistance in producing yet another wonderful book.

Sarah Durdin Robertson and Lisa Harrison deserve recognition for selflessly pouring their hearts and souls into everything they do for me. I'd also like to thank Anna Burges-Lumsden for her continued hard work and support.

James Edgar has my respect for his gifted design and art direction which has led to an appealing and captivating book.

A big thank you to copyeditors Trish Burgess and Miren Lopategui whose attention to detail is second to none.

The fabulous images throughout the book are the work of photographer Con Poulos and stylist Elodie Rambaud, whose flair is apparent in every picture.

I would like to thank One Potato Two Potato for producing another brilliant series, especially Pat Llewellyn, Ben Adler, Sue Murphy, Paul Ratcliffe, Melanie Bones, Colin Steele, Anna Horsburgh and Miranda Sherriff. I am so proud of this team whose energy and enthusiasm never flounders.

Thanks also to Charles Walker at United Agents.

Lastly, I would like to mention Jennifer Aves-Elliott, my assistant, whose extraordinary skills and patience enable me to achieve so much of what I do. I remain eternally grateful.

MANAGING DIRECTOR Pat Llewellyn
SERIES PRODUCER & DIRECTOR Paul Ratcliffe
HEAD OF POTATOES Sarah Durdin Robertson
ASSISTANT FOOD PRODUCER Anna Horsburgh